# Kaypro®
# User's Handbook

# KAYPRO®
# USER'S HANDBOOK

Weber Systems Inc. Staff

Ballantine Books • New York

**Kaypro® User's Handbook**



Library of Congress Catalog Card Number: 83-91205
ISBN 0-345-31595-2

Manufactured in the United States of America

First Ballantine Books Edition: February 1984
10 9 8 7 6 5 4 3 2 1

# CONTENTS

# CHAPTER 1.
# INTRODUCTION TO THE KAYPRO II AND ITS SOFTWARE

## INTRODUCTION

This book contains an explanation of the Kaypro II computer, its software, and peripheral devices.

This book's first chapter contains an overview of the features of the Kaypro II and its software. This chapter also contains a discussion of the installation and operation of the computer.

The second chapter contains an introduction to CP/M (Control Program/Monitor). CP/M is an operating system which controls the input and output operations of the computer.

Chapters 3 through 8 include an explanation of the various software packages which are included with the Kaypro II computer. The word processor (Perfect Writer), speller (Perfect Speller and Word+), spreadsheet (Perfect Calc), database (Perfect Filer), and financial program (Profit Plan) are all covered in these chapters.

The last two chapters contain an explanation of programming the Kaypro II computer. Chapter 9 is dedicated to programming with Microsoft BASIC, while Chapter 10 explains the use of S-BASIC.

## SPECIFICATIONS

The Kaypro II computer is a completely self-contained desktop computer. The keyboard and main computer consoles are the only items necessary for a wide range of applications.

The Kaypro II consists of a keyboard console and main computer console, as depicted in Illustration 1-1.

**Illustration 1-1. Kaypro II Computer Consoles**

**FRONT:** 1. Monitor 2. Power Indicator 3. Disk Drives
4. Numeric Keypad 5. Keyboard

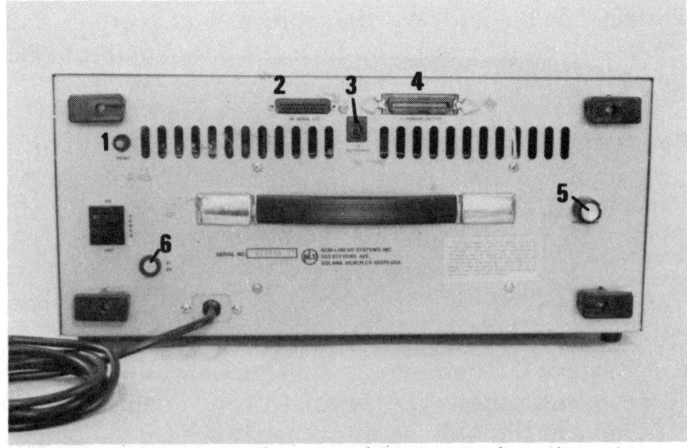


**BACK:** 1. Reset Switch 2. Serial Port 3. Keyboard Cord Jack
4. Parallel Port 5. Intensity Control Knob
6. Fuse Holder

The keyboard console consists of a typewriter style keyboard and a numeric keypad.

The main computer console contains the majority of the electronic components of the computer. This includes the CPU (Central Processing Unit) as well as the RAM (Random Access Memory) and the ROM (Read Only Memory). The main console also includes the power switch, the reset switch, the display intensity control and three jacks for connections to external devices. Finally, the monitor (video display) is included with two floppy disk drives in the main console.

The keyboard console and the main computer console are connected together with a standard, coiled telephone cord.

## CPU

The central processing unit is an electronic circuit which performs calculations and manipulates data in the computer. The CPU can be thought of as the "brains" of the computer system.

The fundamental component of a CPU is one or more microprocessors. A microprocessor is an electronic device that performs operations as specified by a set of instructions. The instructions are in the form of machine language. Machine language is the only set of instructions that a microprocessor understands.

Several different types of microprocessors are commonly used in modern computers. The CPU used in the Kaypro II contains the popular Z-80 microprocessor.

Although microprocessors understand machine language, people generally do not. As a result, high level programming languages are generally used to write programs. A high level language is a set of instructions that are easy for people to understand. S-BASIC and Microsoft BASIC are two examples of high level languages.

The conversion from a high level language to machine language is either done with an interpreter or a compiler. A compiler is a program that converts an entire high level program to machine language. A compiler performs a complete translation of the set of instructions before the program is actually executed. An interpreter converts each instruction to machine language as the program is executed.

A compiled language such as S-BASIC executes programs very quickly. However, an interpreted language such as Microsoft BASIC is easier to use, because it does not need to be compiled. Unfortunately, interpreted languages require more time to execute because each instruction must be translated into machine language as the program proceeds.

**RAM**

The CPU cannot perform any operations or process any data unless a set of instructions (a program) and data are provided. The part of the computer that is used to store programs and data is called the random access memory, or RAM. The CPU processes the data that is stored in RAM. As a result, computers with more random access memory can handle longer programs and more data than computers with less RAM.

A convenient unit of memory capacity is the kilobyte, or simply K. One K is enough memory capacity to store 1024 character of data, or about one-half of a typed page. Generally, small computers contain 16K, 32K, 48K, 64K, or 128K of RAM.

The Kaypro II has 64K of RAM. This is roughly enough memory to store 30 typed pages of information (double-spaced).

The random access memory cannot be maintained unless the computer is powered on. As a result, the contents of RAM are erased when the power is shut off.

An additional 2K of RAM are provided with the Kaypro II to control the video display.

## ROM

Read-Only Memory is similar in principle to RAM, but has two distinct features. The contents of the read-only memory cannot be changed. Also, the contents of ROM remain intact when the computer is shut off.

This set of "indelible" instructions are used by the computer to maintain operations. Since the Kaypro II contains only 2K of ROM, the computer can do very little until it receives more instructions.

## Storing Information On Diskettes

Since the program and data memory of the computer is erased each time the computer is shut off, another method of storing programs and data is required. Some computer systems include either "hard" disks or Winchester disks. Both of these systems can be used to store large amounts of information, but they are generally too expensive for small computer applications. Low cost cassette tape storage devices are also available, but these units are generally inconvenient and can only store a limited amount of data.

As a result, small computer systems generally use a "floppy" disk system. A floppy diskette is depicted in Illustration 1-3.

Floppy disk systems are much more convenient than cassette tape units and not as expensive as Winchester or hard disk systems.

Floppy diskettes got their name because they are, in fact, quite flexible. They generally consist of a circular magnetic surface protected by a square plastic cover. Both 5¼ inch and 8 inch floppy diskettes are common. As expected, 8 inch diskettes can store more information than 5¼ inch diskettes.

The Kaypro II computer is supplied with two 5¼ inch disk drives. Each of these disk drives are capable of recording 191K of information on a diskette. The complete description of the Kaypro II disk system is a two drive, single sided, double density, soft sectored mini-diskette system. The exact nature of the disk system is described later in this chapter.

### Printers

Two types of printers are commonly used with modern computer equipment. These two types, serial and parallel, differ mainly in the format that the computer sends data to the printer. The Kaypro II is designed to be used with a parallel printer. The speed and accuracy of parallel printers make them much more popular than serial printers.

Most parallel printers use a standard "Centronics" connector. This connector allows most parallel printers to be connected directly to the "PRINTER OUTPUT" jack on the Kaypro. However, you should insist on a demonstration before purchasing a printer.

### Modems

RS-232 is the name of a standardized method used to send and receive data. A modem is a device that is used to transmit and receive data using telephone lines. Nearly all modems operate acording to the specifications of RS-232.

Since the serial port on the Kaypro II complies to the RS-232 standard, most modems can be connected directly to the Kaypro II.

## SOFTWARE

Software is a term that is used to describe the intangible aspects of the computer system. On the other hand, hardware is a term that describes the physical devices included in a computer system.

Software is divided into three general categories: operating systems, languages, and applications programs.

## Operating Systems

An operating system is a program that controls the actual operation of the computer. An operating system is a set of instructions that are used to manipulate data. The operating system also controls the input and output of the computer, as well as the I/O (input/output) devices.

The I/O devices of a computer are the equipment that allow the computer to accept or provide information. A keyboard, video display, and printer are all examples of I/O devices.

In general, an operating system is a set of instructions that determine how the computer works. CP/M is the operating system that is used with the Kaypro II computer.

CP/M was developed by Digital Research. It has become a very popular operating system for small computers with disk drives. CP/M Version 2.2 is supplied with the Kaypro II.

A wide range of applications programs are available for systems that have the CP/M operating system. Since CP/M is standard, most of these programs can be used with the Kaypro II.

## Languages

Languages are programs that convert a set of instructions into machine language. Most programming languages (BASIC, FORTRAN, PASCAL, etc.) have straightforward and easy to understand instructions. However, the computer cannot execute these instructions unless they are reduced to machine language (a set of instructions which a microprocessor can execute).

Two types of programs can be used to translate a programming language to machine language. These programs are interpreters and compilers.

As previously mentioned, a compiler is used to translate a complete program into machine language. This requires a separate compilation step before the program can be executed. S-BASIC is a compiled languaged used with the Kaypro II.

An interpreter is used to convert individual instructions into machine language while the program is executing. Since the translation occurs during execution, interpreted languages generally require more time to complete a program. Microsoft BASIC is an interpreted languaged included in the Kaypro II software package.

## Applications Programs

Applications programs are a set of instructions that allow the computer to perform a useful function. Accounting programs, word processors, and forecasting programs are available from a wide range of vendors. However, if a specific application requires software that is not available, the software must be developed by the user.

It is generally very expensive and time consuming to create a custom made applications program. As a result, many people choose the applications programs they need before they choose a computer to run the programs.

The software provided with the Kaypro II computer includes an excellent set of applications programs. The word processing programs, Perfect Writer, Perfect Speller, and Word Plus, provide an easy method to create and edit as well as check the spelling of documents.

A filing system, Perfect Filer, provides an easy method to create and maintain files.

Perfect Calc is a program that generates a spreadsheet. This is basically a table of values that can be manipulated mathematically. This spreadsheet is useful for financial, as well as scientific, or any type of calculations.

Profit Plan is similar in concept to Perfect Calc. However, Profit Plan provides more features for generating tables and reports.

A set of assorted game programs are also provided on the Microsoft BASIC diskette.

The software provided with the Kaypro II is summarized in Table 1-1.

**Table 1-1. Kaypro II Software**

| | |
|---|---|
| **Operating System:** | CP/M Version 2.2 |
| **Languages:** | Microsoft BASIC (Interpreted)<br>S-BASIC (Compiled) |
| **Applications Programs:** | Perfect Writer<br>Perfect Speller<br>Word Plus<br>Perfect Filer<br>Perfect Calc<br>Profit Plan |

The standard Kaypro software package is subject to change. If you do not already own a Kaypro computer, be sure that you consult your computer dealer for the software package currently offered.

## HARDWARE

The Kaypro II computer equipment consists of two items: the main computer console and the keyboard console (as depicted in Illustration 1-1).

The keyboard, numeric keypad, monitor, and disk drives are the four principle devices for the input and output of the computer system.

## Keyboard

The Kaypro II keyboard and numeric keypad are depicted in Illustration 1-2.

**Illustration 1-2. Kaypro II Keyboard and Numeric Keypad**

The keyboard is similar in many respects to a standard typewriter keyboard. However, the computer contains several keys that are not generally found on a typewriter. These keys (CTRL, ESC, ↓ ,etc.) are used to perform special functions in the different modes of operation of the computer.

The keys on the upper right hand of the keyboard (←,→, ↑, and ↓ ) are used to control the cursor. The cursor is an indicator of where the next character will be displayed on the screen. On the Kaypro II computer, the cursor is a blinking underline character. Different computers may use a different symbol as the cursor.

The CTRL key is used in a similar manner as the SHIFT key. when the SHIFT key is depressed, most of the other keys on the keyboard represent a different character. Similarly, when the CTRL key is depressed, many keys have a unique function. The CTRL key has no results when it is used by itself. The CTRL key is always used along with another key.

The function of the ESC key is slightly different. The ESC key is also used to generate different functions for the keys, but the ESC key is not used at the same time as another key. The ESC key is sometimes used by itself, and sometimes followed by another key. The exact function of the ESC key depends on the current mode of the computer.

### Numeric Keypad

The smaller keypad to the right of the main computer is provided as a more convenient means of entering numeric data. The keys on the keypad have exactly the same function as the keys with the same markings on the main keyboard. The Enter key has the same function as the Return key.

### Monitor

The video display of the computer is generally called the monitor. The monitor is used as a means for the computer to display information. Numbers, letters, and other special characters appear on the CRT (Cathode Ray Tube). The characters appear green on a dark background. The intensity of the characters on the display is controlled by an adjustment knob on the back of the computer (some models my have the intensity control on the front). The monitor can display 24 lines of information with up to 80 characters on each line. The 9 inch diagonal display allows the information to be easily read from the monitor.

### Disk Drives

The disk drives are the components that provide the versatility of the computer system. The large amount of data that can be stored on a diskette makes it a very important element of the computer system.

## Floppy Diskettes

The most widely used type of disk storage with microcomputers is floppy disk storage. A floppy diskette consists of a round vinyl disk which is enclosed within a plastic cover. The diskette is generally stored in a diskette envelope.

This cover protects the diskette from damage while it is being handled by the operator. The diskette should never be removed from its cover. A 5¼ inch diskette with its protective envelope is shown in Illustration 1-3.

The diskette is allowed to rotate within the protective cover. The round hole in the middle of the diskette allows the disk drive to hold the diskette and spin it. The oblong shaped opening on the protective envelope provides an area where the head can read from or write to the diskette surface.

**Illustration 1-3. Mini-Floppy Diskette**

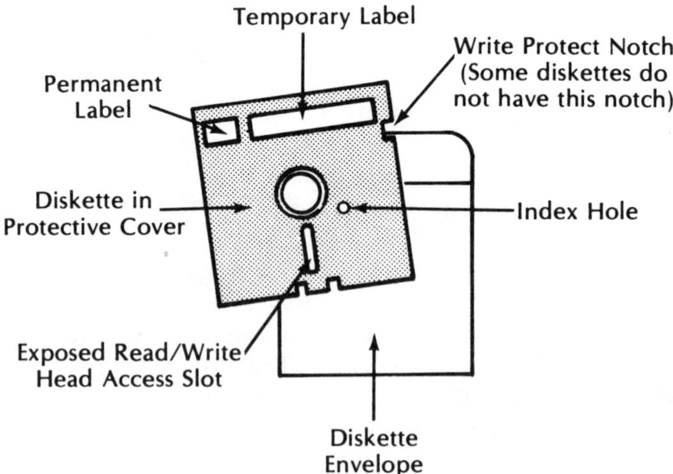

**Tracks and Sectors**

To facilitate the process of searching for data on the diskette surface, the surface is divided into tracks and sectors.

Tracks may be visualized as a series of concentric circles on the diskette surface, as shown in Illustration 1-4. There are 40 tracks on a diskette used by the Kaypro II.

To further reduce the time necessary to search for a particular data item, the tracks are divided into sectors, which are also shown in Illustration 1-4.

**Illustration 1-4. Tracks and Sectors**

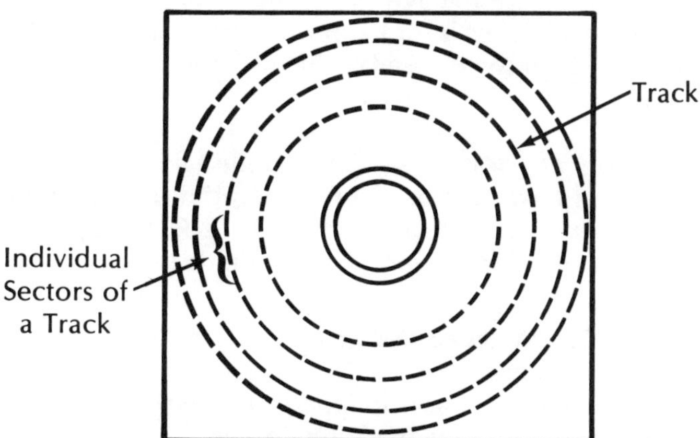


**Locating Tracks and Sectors**

Locating a particular track on the disk surface is a relatively uncomplicated matter. The drive merely moves the head to the position on the diskette where the specified track is located, much like the needle on a phonograph is positioned to the location of a specific song on a record album.

However, locating a particular sector is a more difficult process. An index hole is used to determine the position of the diskette. It is located just to the right of the large hole in the middle of the 5¼ inch diskette.

The index hole, as shown in Illustration 1-3, is a hole only in the diskette's protective covering. Another index hole is located on the actual diskette surface inside the envelope. As the diskette spins, the index hole on the diskette surface passes underneath the hole in the protective envelope.

A light source inside the disk drive shines light onto the area of the diskette containing the index hole. When an index hole on the disk surface is aligned with the index hole on the protective envelope, the light will shine through to a sensor. The sensor will relay information on the location of the index hole, which can be used to calculate the various sector locations.

This method of locating sectors is called soft sectoring. Although the Kaypro II uses soft sectored diskettes, some computers use a similar system called hard sectoring. Hard sectored diskettes have more than one index hole.

### Single and Double Sided Diskettes

Some floppy diskettes are designed to be written on only one side. These are known as single sided (SS) diskettes.

Diskettes which are designed to be written on both sides are known as double sided (DS) diskettes.

### Single, Double, and Quad Density Diskettes

Density refers to a diskette's recording format, which in turn affects its capacity. Single density 5¼ inch diskettes have roughly 94K of capacity, double density 5¼ inch diskettes have a capacity of about 150-200K, and quad density 5¼ inch diskettes have a capacity of up to 370K.

The Kaypro II computer uses single sided double density diskettes. A small amount of the storage capacity of each diskette is reserved for the operations of the disk drives. The available storage capacity of each diskette is 191K.

**Diskette Write Protection**

Diskettes have a notch on the side of their protective envelope which determines whether or not data can be written onto that diskette. On 8 inch diskettes, this notch is known as a write-protect notch. On 5¼ inch diskettes, it is known as a write-enable notch.

On an 8 inch diskette, information cannot be written onto the diskette unless this notch has been covered. On 5¼ inch diskettes, information cannot be written onto the diskette unless the notch is left uncovered.

Some 5¼ inch diskettes may be permanently write protected if their protective envelope does not contain a notch. Any 5¼ inch diskette with a notch can be write protected by merely covering the notch with a piece of tape as shown in Illustration 1-5.

**Illustration 1-5. Write Protecting a 5¼ Inch Diskette**

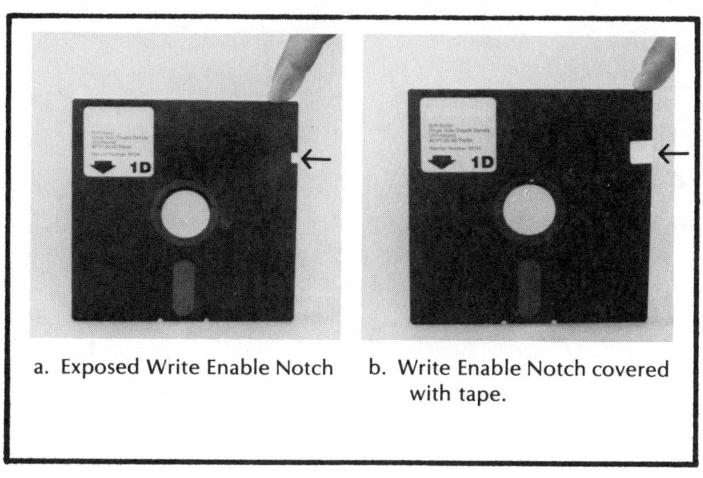


a. Exposed Write Enable Notch

b. Write Enable Notch covered with tape.

## Inserting and Removing Diskettes

Be sure to remove any diskettes before the Kaypro's power is turned on or off. Furthermore, a diskette should never be removed from a disk drive while the disk drive is operating. At any other time, diskettes can be readily inserted and removed from the disk drives.

Before a diskette can be inserted, the drive door must be open. As depicted in Illustration 1-6, the drive door can be opened by gently pulling the bottom of the door forward.

**Illustration 1-6. Opening a Disk Drive Door**

A diskette should be inserted into a disk drive with the head access slot forward and on top (see Illustration 1-7). The diskette label should be on the top also. If the diskette has a write enable notch, this should be on the left edge.

**Illustration 1-7. Inserting a Diskette**

The disk drive will not operate unless the drive door is closed. The door can be closed by gently pressing down the front of the door. If the door does not close all the way, the diskette is probably not all the way in the drive.

Diskettes are removed from the disk drives simply by lifting the door and pulling the diskette out of the drive.

## SETTING UP

The Kaypro II computer should be set up in an area where it will not be exposed to extreme heat, cold, or humidity. Also, be sure to keep the computer dry at all times. The computer should be placed on a firm, flat surface, away from hazards.

Be sure that the power switch (on the back of the console) is in the Off position before proceeding.

The power cord that enters the back of the console should be plugged into a standard wall outlet. Avoid connecting the computer to the same circuit as other heavy electrical equipment. Also, avoid connecting the computer to an outlet that is controlled by a wall switch. Connect the computer to a circuit that is unlikely to be disturbed in any way.

Position the computer so the display is in the viewing direction. Be sure that there is enough room for the keyboard in an appropriate place. It is often convenient to "prop up" the front of the main computer console on the back of the keyboard console, as depicted in Illustration 1-8.

**Illustration 1-8. Typical Kaypro II Setup**

Insert either end of the coiled cord into the jack labeled J3 KEYBOARD on the back of the main computer console. The tab on the plug is used to latch the plug in the jack. Be sure that the tab is on the top, and insert the plug until the latch "clicks" into place (see Illustration 1-9a).

Insert the other end of the cord into the keyboard console. The plug fits into the jack in the same manner, but the tab on the plug should be on the bottom (see Illustration 1-9b).

Be sure to remove the protective cardboard from the disk drives. The cardboard is labeled "REMOVE THIS AT OPERATION".

**Illustration 1-9. Inserting Keyboard Cord**

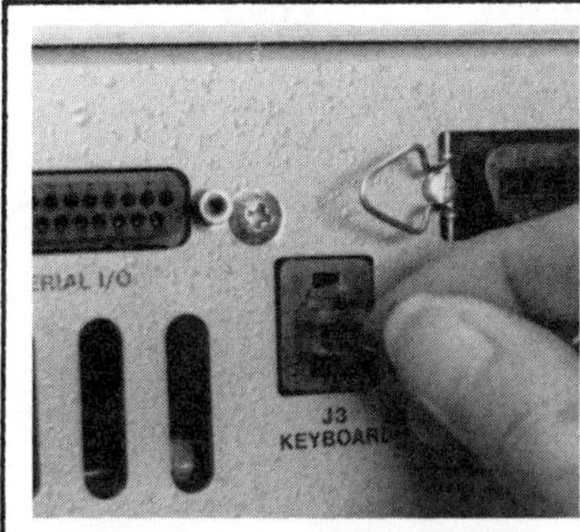


a. Inserting keyboard cord to main computer console.

b. Inserting keyboard cord to keyboard console.

## POWERING ON

When the setup of the computer console is complete, turn on the power switch on the back of the main computer console.

The power indicator on the front panel should glow red, and both disk drives should begin operating. The red light adjacent to disk drive A should also glow.

After several seconds, the following display appears on the screen:

```
*  KAYPRO II  *

Please insert your diskette into Drive A
```

Obtain the diskette labeled Master #1, CP/M Version 2.2 and insert it into drive A. When the drive door is closed, the disk drive continues to operate momentarily, then stops. The following message then appears on the display:

```
KAYPRO II
64k CP/M v 2.2

A>_
```

The prompt A> is displayed as a signal that the computer is ready to execute a CP/M command. An introduction to CP/M and the most common CP/M commands can be found in Chapter 2.

There are several CP/M commands that are very useful. However, there are only a few that are absolutly essential. The first operations that any user performs on the Kaypro II computer is duplicating the set of master diskettes using CP/M commands.

The procedure for duplicating the set of master diskettes is simple and easy to follow. Be sure to consult the next chapter for instructions on how to duplicate the master diskettes.

# CHAPTER 2.
# BASIC CP/M OPERATION

## INTRODUCTION

CP/M is the operating system for the Kaypro computer. This chapter provides the information necessary to manipulate files using CP/M commands.

This chapter is intended to cover only the aspects of CP/M needed for general use of the Kaypro computer. If your interest in CP/M exceeds the scope of this book, consult *CP/M Simplified* also by Weber Systems, Inc.

The CP/M commands are generally used to create and edit files, list files on the display or printer, copy files on another diskette or erase files.

## DUPLICATING MASTER DISKETTES

The diskettes provided with the Kaypro computer are very valuable. As a result, the master diskettes should be copied and put in a safe place.

The first step is to obtain enough high quality diskettes to make a copy of each diskette that is provided with the Kaypro computer. Be sure to use single sided, soft sectored, double density mini-floppy diskettes.

Also, be sure to label all diskettes as soon as they are copied. Once a label is applied to a diskette, do not write on the label with a ball point pen. Always use a felt tip pen when writing on diskettes. The pressure of a ball point pen can damage the surface of a diskette.

## Formatting

The Kaypro computer cannot use a diskette unless the information on the diskette is in the correct format. The FORMAT command is used to erase the contents of a diskette (if any), and prepare the diskette to be used with the Kaypro.

Turn on the computer and insert the CP/M diskette as described in the previous chapter. When the CP/M prompt (A>) appears, type FORMAT, followed by Return.

A> FORMAT ↵*

In response to this command, a list of selections called a menu appears.

Insert the diskette that you would like to format in the disk drive labeled B. Press F on the keyboard, followed by Return, to begin the format procedure.

The computer checks to make sure every track of the diskette is properly formatted. If a problem occurs, choose selection F on the menu again to repeat the procedure, or choose selection S to reformat one track.

When the S selection is chosen, respond again with the track number where the problem occurred.

When the format procedure is complete, the menu is again displayed on the monitor. If you would like to format another diskette, remove the diskette from drive B and repeat the FORMAT procedure.

When enough blank diskettes have been formatted for the entire set of master diskettes, choose selection E from the menu to return to CP/M.

---

*↵ indicates pressing the Return key.
__ indicate characters which are entered by the operator.

## Copying

To copy the master diskettes, be sure that the CP/M diskette is in drive A. In response to the CP/M prompt, type COPY followed by Return.

A> COPY

The COPY command also displays a menu on the display.

Replace the CP/M diskette in drive A with the diskette that you wish to copy. Insert a blank, formatted diskette in drive B.

For copying important diskettes, choose selection C. Selection F can also be used to copy diskettes, but this selection does not verify that the two copies are identical.

Observe the results of the verify procedure. If an error occurs, format the diskette in drive B again, then repeat the copy/verify procedure. Keep repeating these steps until all of the master diskettes (including the CP/M diskette) are copied accurately.

## Generating Working Diskettes

A **working diskette** is a diskette that contains a copy of the operating system.

Up to this point, the only diskette that could be used to start up the system was the CP/M diskette. The other diskettes could not be used because they did not contain the CP/M program. Since the computer is helpless without CP/M, the diskette in drive A must always be a CP/M diskette, or contain a copy of CP/M.

The SYSGEN command can be used to copy the operating system onto any diskette without eliminating the previous information on the diskette.

As a preventive measure, all of the master diskettes are "write-protected". As a result, SYSGEN cannot be used to copy CP/M onto any master diskette.

The SYSGEN command allows the copied diskettes to be used by themselves, in drive A. This allows drive B to be used with additional diskettes.

In order to copy the operating system onto the newly made copies, insert the CP/M diskette in drive A. Insert the copy diskette into drive B, and enter the following underlined statements.

```
A> SYSGEN
KAYPRO SYSGEN VER 2.2
SOURCE DRIVE NAME (OR RETURN TO SKIP) A
SOURCE ON A, THEN TYPE RETURN
FUNCTION COMPLETE
DESTINATION DRIVE NAME (OR RETURN TO REBOOT) B
DESTINATION ON B, THEN TYPE RETURN
FUNCTION COMPLETE
DESTINATION DRIVE NAME (OR RETURN TO REBOOT)
```

If you wish to make working copies of several diskettes, this procedure can be repeated. When the complete set of diskettes have a copy of CP/M on them, press the Return key in response to the DESTINATION prompt. This causes a return to CP/M.

Now that the master diskettes are copied, put them in a safe place, and do not use them unless additional copies are needed.

From this point, use only the working copies of the diskettes with the computer.

It is generally a good idea to format additional blank diskettes for miscellaneous files.

## FILES

A **file** on a diskette is analogous to a file in a filing cabinet. A file is simply a place to store information. Each file on a diskette has a name that distinguishes it from the other files. A filename consists of two parts, the primary name and the extension. The primary name can contain up to 8 characters, and the extension can have up to three characters. The primary name must be separated from the extension by a period (.).

The following filenames are suitable for the Kaypro computer:

PROGRAM.BAS
DUMP.COM
SBIOS.ASM
%%%.↑↑

Generally, the primary name is used to specify the file, and the extension is used to describe the type of information in the file.

Some commonly used filename extensions are listed in Table 2-1.

**Table 2-1. Typical Filename Extensions**

| | |
|---|---|
| COM | CP/M Command |
| BAS | BASIC Program |
| ASM | Assembly Language Program |
| BAK | Backup File |
| DAT | Data File |

### Filename Match Characters

Match characters are sometimes called "wildcards" because they are used to represent any characters in a filename.

The question mark (?) is a match character that represents a single character in a filename. The asterisk (*) represents a group of characters in a filename.

For example, if a CP/M command includes the filename,

FILE?.BAS

the following files would all be affected:

FILE1.BAS
FILEA.BAS
FILE#.BAS

If a CP/M command includes the filename,

FILE*.BAS

the following files would be affected:

FILENO.BAS
FILE.BAS
FILENAME.BAS
FILE123.BAS

As would be expected, the filename *.* matches every file.

**System Prompt**

The prompt A> that appears on the display is a signal that the computer is ready to accept a CP/M command.

The prompt is also used to specify the disk drive currently in use. The prompt can be changed by keying in the following command:

A>B: ↵

The system prompt would subsequently appear as the following:

B>

Disk drive A is said to be the default drive when the system prompt is A>. Disk drive B is the default drive when the prompt is B>.

### Warm Boot

Warm boot (or warm start) is a term that describes the restarting of the operating system.

A warm boot occurs automatically after many operations of the computer. When this occurs, the Warm Boot message appears on the display screen.

A warm boot can also be generated by holding down the CTRL key while pressing the C key. This interrupts whatever the computer has been doing, restarts the operating system, and displays the system prompt.

A warm boot is a good way to get out of a problem situation on the computer. Control-C is generally used to stop a program that begins to go wrong.

When a diskette is removed from a disk drive and another is inserted, a warm boot must be executed before data can be written on the diskette. A warm boot is a means for the disk drive to become acquainted with the diskette. When a new disk is inserted, the diskette can be read, but data cannot be written to the diskette until a warm boot is performed.

### Disk Directory

The DIR command is used to obtain a list of the files on a diskette. For example, insert a copy of the CP/M diskette in drive A and press the reset switch on the back of the computer console. When the system prompt A> is displayed, enter the DIR command.

A> DIR

The list of files on the diskette is displayed as follows.

```
A: MOVCPM   COM : PIP      COM : SUBMIT  COM : XSUB      COM
A: ED       COM : ASM      COM : DDT     COM : STAT      COM
A: SYSGEN   COM : DUMP     ASM : COPY    COM : FORMAT    COM
A: BAUD     COM : TERM     COM : SBASIC  COM : OVERLAYB  COM
A: BASICLIB REL : USERLIB  REL : FAC     BAS : XAMN      BAS
A: DPLAY    BAS : CONFIG   COM : LOAD    COM : DUMP      COM
A: SBIOS    ASM : DISKDEF  LIB
```

The DIR command can also be used to locate specific files. If a file is specified in a DIM command, only the name (or names) that match the specified filename are listed.

For example, given the preceding directory, the command:

A> DIR *.BAS

would have the following results:

```
A: FAC      BAS  : XAMN   BAS  : DPLAY   BAS
```

If no files match the specified filename, the following message is displayed:

NO FILE

If a diskette is present in drive B, the command,

A> DIR B:

would generate the directory of that diskette.

An alternative way to produce the directory of the diskette in drive B is to make B the default drive, and simply enter DIR instead of DIR B:.

For example,

A > B:
B > DIR

has the same results as A > DIR B:.

### Creating and Editing Files

CP/M includes a text editor for creating and altering files. However, it is much easier to edit files using the word processor (Perfect Writer) than the ED command.

The first step in creating or editing a file is to enter ED followed by a filename.

A > ED PROGRAM1.BAS

If PROGRAM1.BAS already existed on the diskette in drive A, then the preceding command would make that program file available for ED.

If PROGRAM1.BAS did not already exist on the diskette, then CP/M would assume that you wanted to create a new file with the filename PROGRAM1.BAS.

If this was the case, ED would respond to your initial entry with the following:

```
NEW FILE
      : *
```

This message means that CP/M will create the new file on the diskette in drive A.

### Entering New Text With I

After the ED command has been entered with an appropriate filename, an asterisk (*) will appear at the end of the next line. This asterisk lets you know that ED is ready to use.

To begin entering text into the file, the Insert command must be entered, as shown below:

After the Insert command has been entered, the ED prompt character will disappear, and you can begin entering text into the edit buffer by typing on the keyboard. The edit buffer is the area of the computer's memory where the actual editing of files occurs.

Once you have finished inserting text into the edit buffer, you must notify the ED program that you wish to terminate the Insert command. This is done by pressing the Z key while holding down the Control key (Control-Z or ↑Z). After Control-Z has been pressed, the Edit prompt will reappear.

At this point, you may wish to review the text you have just entered to check for errors. You can display the entire edit buffer by entering the following command:

*B#T

The B command moves ED back to the beginning of the edit buffer while the #T types out the lines in the edit buffer until the end of the file has been reached.

The following example contains an S-BASIC program with the filename PROGRAM1.BAS. The underlined entries are the user's responses.

**Example**

```
A> ED PROGRAM1.BAS

NEW FILE
   : *I
  1:  VAR X = INTEGER
  2:  REPEAT
  3:    BEGIN
  4:      X = X + 1
  5:      PRINT X
  6:    END
  7:  UNTIL X = 100
  8:  ↑Z
   : *E

Warm Boot

A>
```

In order for a file to be saved on a diskette, the End command (E) must be used to exit the edit mode. In the preceding example, E is the last command entered. The End command saves the file and returns the computer to the CP/M command level.

Editing files requires the use of the Append command. The Append command copies lines from the file being edited into the edit buffer. An example of the Append command is given below:

```
: *10A
```

The number preceding the Append command specifies the number of lines from the file being edited to be appended to the edit buffer.

The Insert command is used to replace any lines of the files that need to be changed. As demonstrated in the following example, Control-Z is used once again to exit the Insert mode.

The Kill command (K) is used to eliminate the incorrect line from the file.

**Example**

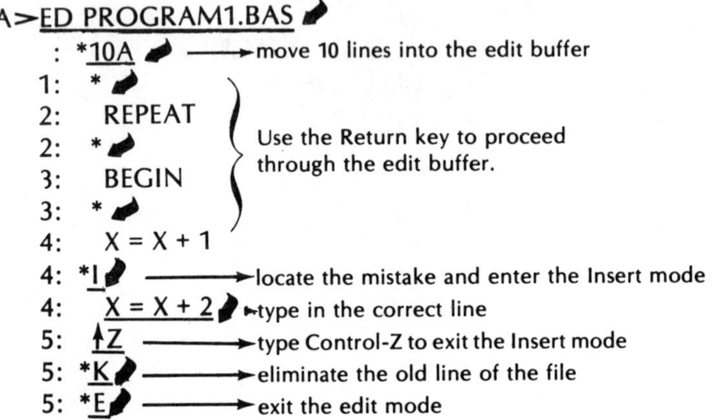


Warm Boot

A>

The ED command requires some practice before it can be used efficiently. Fortunately, the Perfect Writer program makes editing files much easier.

## Renaming a File

The REN (Rename) command is used to change a file's name. It takes the following form:

REN new name = old name

For example, if the data file ACCT.DAT resides on the diskette in drive A, the filename can be changed to NAME.DAT with the following statement.

A>REN NAME.DAT = ACCT.DAT

**Copying a File**

Whenever you obtain or create a new program or data file, you should make a copy of it immediately. Store your master diskette is a safe place and use your copies for day to day operation.

Also, when you are updating a file, you should make a copy of that updated file before leaving the system. Be sure to label the copy and record its date.

The PIP command is used in CP/M to copy files. PIP is an abbreviation for Peripheral Interchange Program. PIP is a program written in machine language that resides on the CP/M diskette.

Let's assume that the CP/M diskette is in drive A, and contains the data file ACCT.DAT. When the system prompt is displayed, PIP can be executed by entering the following command:

```
A>PIP
*
```

The asterisk is PIP's program prompt and tells the user that PIP is executing.

Your next step is to type in the PIP expression that will perform the desired copying. Such PIP expressions take the following form:

d:*copyname* = d:*originalname*

In the above expression, d stands for the letter of the disk drive. *copyname* and *originalname* respectively stand for the names of the file to be created as the copy, and the actual existing file from which the copy is to be made.

For example, the following example,

*B:ACCT.BAK = A:NAME.DAT

tells PIP to make a copy of NAME.DAT on drive A and to name this copy ACCT.BAK, placing it on drive B.

After the copy operation has finished, the PIP prompt will appear as follows:

*

If you press the Return key, you will exit PIP, giving control back to the operating system.

*

Warm Boot

Regardless of which drive was copied to or from, PIP will always return to the drive from which you originally executed the command. Since PIP was originally executed from drive A in our example, that is the drive to which it will return.

The disk drive lights will go on and off as PIP is copying a file. That is due to the fact that PIP copies the files in segments called blocks. If the file is lengthy, PIP must keep going back to the original file to get more blocks. This is the reason why the disk drive lights will blink on and off.

Returning to our example, we had a copy of the file named ACCT.DAT which was renamed NAME.DAT on drive A. Suppose we now wish to make a copy of NAME.DAT on drive B. We would use the following command to do this:

A > PIP B:NAME.DAT = A:NAME.DAT

Notice that we used the same name for the new file as was used for the original file. When using the same filename for both the copy and the original, it is not necessary to name the copy's filename in your command. The following command would then be the equivalent of the command given earlier:

A>PIP B: = A:NAME.DAT ⏎

Remember, you cannot have two files on the same diskette with the same name. If you attempted to copy NAME.DAT without specifying a new drive or new name, the following statement would appear:

DISK WRITE ERROR: (error)

In actual usage, the expression causing the error will replace the (error) in the preceding statement.

**Printing Files**

You are now ready to learn to send a copy of a file to the printer. There are two different methods of doing so in CP/M.

One method is to use the CTRL and P keys along with the TYPE command. first of all, press the CTRL (Control) key and P key (↑P) simultaneously. Now, whatever you type at the keyboard will be displayed on the screen as well as printed by the printer. Before using Control-P, be sure that your printer is turned on.

After having entered Control-P (↑P), you can now enter a TYPE command at the keyboard to list a file on the printer. This is shown in the following example.

```
A > TYPE PROGRAM1.BAS
VAR X = INTEGER
REPEAT
 BEGIN
  X = X + 2
  PRINT X
 END
UNTIL X = 100

A>
```

The file PROGRAM1.BAS will be displayed on your screen and simultaneously printed by your line printer when the above command is entered while Control-P is active.

If you press Control-P again, you will deactivate the printer. If you use the TYPE command when the printer is not active, the file will only be displayed on the video screen. It will not be listed on the printer.

The second method of printing files uses the LPT: device name. This is generally more efficient than using Control-P with the TYPE command, especially if you wish to print several files.

An example of the use of the LPT: is given below:

```
A > PIP LPT: = PROGRAM1.BAS
```

This command sends the file PROGRAM1.BAS to the listing device, in our case the printer.

### Erasing Files

Suppose that you had the file ACCT.BAK on both drive A and drive B, and you wished to erase the file on drive A. First of all, before erasing any files, check your directory to see which files you have on the diskette in drive A.

A>DIR

Next, use the DIR command to list the files on the diskette on drive B.

A>DIR B:

You can now issue an ERA command that will erase ACCT.BAK in drive A as illustrated below:

A>ERA ACCT.BAK

If you wish to erase several or all of the files on a diskette, you can do so by using a filename match as illustrated below:

A>ERA ACCT.*

This will erase all files on drive A with the filename ACCT regardless of what that file's filename extension is.

The CP/M commands introduced in this chapter are not necessary for the general use of the Kaypro computer.

However, from time to time, the CP/M commands make the operations of the computer much easier.

Don't be discouraged if the CP/M commands seem confusing. The applications programs provided with the Kaypro are generally much easier to understand.

# CHAPTER 3.
# PERFECT WRITER

## INTRODUCTION

Perfect Writer is a word processing program which is included in the standard software package of the Kaypro computer. Perfect Writer is a product of Perfect Software, Inc. This word processing program makes creating and editing of documents a simple procedure.

A lessons diskette is also included in the software package. This diskette provides step-by-step instructions on the use of the word processor.

### Concept

The Perfect Writer program has a wide range of capabilities for preparing many types of documents. The set of instructions that are used to manipulate the documents are straightforward and easy to understand.

Each document (letter, memo, program, chapter, etc.) is stored in a file. A file is merely a place where information is stored. The files used by the Perfect Writer are stored on a diskette. Each diskette file is designated by a filename (as described in Chapter 2).

The Perfect Writer program is used to create and edit files. Although the word processor program and the document files can be stored on the same diskette, it is generally a good practice to store the document files on a separate diskette.

When a document is complete, the contents at the document file can be output to a printer that is connected to the computer. The quality of the finished document depends on the type of printer used with the Kaypro.

Although the more expensive printers generally produce the best results, the Perfect Writer program has satisfactory results with inexpensive printers as well.

**Features**

The Perfect Writer program has the ability to generate form letters that are "customized". This not only includes names and addresses, but sections of the document as well. A letter can be modified to include a specific opening, closing, etc., depending on who the letter is sent to.

The word processing program also allows any format for a document. Headings, quotations, verses, lists, footnotes, etc., can all be generated automatically. The program is also capable of accomodating different type styles. Underlined type, bold face, italic, and other type styles can be used (depending on the printer).

Perfect Writer also allows the user to access several documents at once. The display can be used to display two documents at the same time. This feature allows sections of one document to be inserted in another, and vice versa.

Although the computer can only access data that resides in the computer memory, the program allows files that are much larger than the computer's RAM. This is achieved by storing the entire document on a disk file, and only entering a small portion of the file in the computer's memory. As a result, the program is constantly "swapping" the information from the diskette into the computer's memory. This arrangement is called **virtual memory** because the computer can be used as though it has much more memory than it actually does. The virtual memory arrangement allows the Perfect Writer program to be used to edit chapters, or even entire books.

To help organize large documents, the program can be used to generate titles for chapters, headings, sections, etc. As the titles are specified, the program automatically maintains a table of contents. Similarly, an index is automatically maintained for designated topics. Perfect Writer can also manipulate footnotes at the bottom of the page or in a separate section. Footnotes, as well as the index and table of contents are automatically updated as the document is edited.

**Getting Started**

The Perfect Writer master diskette as well as the master lessons diskette and installation diskette should all be promptly copied and placed in a safe place. The "working copy" of each diskette should contain a copy of the operating system. Chapter 2 contains an explanation of the FORMAT, COPY, and SYSGEN commands needed to generate a working copy of each master diskette.

Also, obtain a blank diskette for storing miscellaneous files. Use the FORMAT procedure described in Chapter 2 to prepare the blank diskette.

To begin using the Perfect Writer program, insert the copy of the Edit diskette into drive A and insert the blank, formatted diskette in drive B. Press the Reset switch on the back of the main computer console.

When the system "starts up", the following message appears:

```
KAYPRO II
64k CP/M v 2.2

A>
```

If a different message is displayed on the screen (i.e. Hello There...), the diskette does not contain a copy of the operating system. If this is the case, be sure than you are using a **copy** of the master diskette, then use the SYSGEN command to copy the operating system.

When the system prompt (A>) appears, respond by typing MENU, followed by pressing the Return key.

A>MENU ↵

When this command is entered, the disk drive begins to operate, and the following message appears on the display:

```
Perfect Writer Version 1.03 Main Selection Menu
(c) 1982   Perfect Software, Inc.
```

Below the identification message, a list of selections called a **menu** is displayed. This is the list of functions used with the Perfect Writer program.

## CREATING AND EDITING FILES

To create a file on the diskette, choose selection E (Edit a file) from the menu. It is not necessary to press the Return key when making selections from the menu.

The prompt at the bottom of the screen should appear as follows.

```
Type one character to indicate your selection now.
Your pleasure: (E,F,P,S,D,Z,R,C,X) E
What is the name of the file you wish to edit?
```

In response to this prompt, type the filename that the new document is to be stored in. Be sure to include the prefix B: in front of the filename, to specify the location of the file on the diskette in drive B. For example, make the following entry in response to the prompt:

>B:THANKS ↵

Since there is no file on the diskette in drive B with the name THANKS, a new file is created. As the file is created, the screen is cleared and the following message is displayed at the bottom of the display:

Perfect Writer 1.03 (Fill) thanks: B:THANKS -100%-

This information is called the echo line. This line contains five items of information. The program name (Perfect Writer 1.03), mode (Fill), buffer name (thanks), filename (B:THANKS), and the location within the file. The location is represented by values from 0% (beginning of file) to 100% (end of file).

The small blinking line at the upper left hand corner of the display is the cursor. The cursor is used to indicate where the next character will appear on the display.

Begin entering data in the file by typing the following lines of text. Use the DEL key to correct any mistakes.

Dear Grandma,

Thank you very much for the birthday gift.

Sincerely,

## Saving a File

The file can be saved on the diskette in drive B by holding down the CTRL key and pressing the X key followed by the S key. These keystrokes are represented by the following notation:

Control-X
Control-S

While the file is being saved, the message below the echo line should change from

New File

to

Writing...

and finally to

File Written.

To return to the Perfect Writer menu, press the following keystrokes:

Control-X
Control-C

## Directory

Selection D from the menu is used to "Look at the directory on a disk". A directory is a list of files that are present on a specific diskette.

In order to verify that the file "THANKS" was recorded on the diskette on drive B, press D in response to the menu prompt. The prompt message should appear as follows:

```
Type one character to indicate your selection now.
Your pleasure: (E,F,P,S,D,Z,R,C,X) D
Which drive do you desire a directory of? (e.g. A)
```

Press B to obtain a directory of the diskette in drive B.

The following display appears on the display.

```
Directory for Drive B:

THANKS

Hit any key to return to menu:
```

Once a file has been created and stored on a diskette, it can be retrieved at any time for editing. The same procedure is used to reenter a file as is used to create a file.

## Lessons

The Lessons diskette provides eight lessons for a first time word processor user. These lessons are contained in the following files:

LESSON0
LESSON1
LESSON2
LESSON3
LESSON4
LESSON5
LESSON6
LESSON7

These lessons provide an introduction to the edit features of the Perfect Writer program.

A more concise lesson is provided for experienced word processor users. The file that contains this lesson is called ADVINTRO.

To access the lesson files, insert a working copy of the lessons diskette into disk drive B. Remove the diskette containing the file "THANKS" and place it in a safe place.

Enter E in response to the menu prompt and specify B:LESSON0 as the file to be edited. Advanced users should specify B:ADVINTRO.

If LESSON0 is specified, read the lesson and return to the menu by pressing Control-X, Control-C. Proceed with the subsequent lessons by choosing selection E from the menu and specifying the next numbered lesson. Be sure to include the prefix B:.

## Editing

Editing is the process used to change the contents of a file. The Perfect Writer program has many features which can be used to edit a file quickly and easily.

Most of the editing commands consist of keystrokes that include either the CTRL or ESC keys. Remember that the CTRL (control) key is held down while another key is pressed. On the other hand, the ESC (escape) key is followed by another key.

The notation used here is as follows:

| | |
|---|---|
| Control-X | Hold down the CTRL key and press X. |
| Escape, X | Press ESC, then press X. |

**Cursor Controls**

The keys on the upper right hand section of the keyboard are used to move the cursor around a file in the editor. These keys, ↑, ↓, ←, and → are called the cursor up, cursor down, cursor left, and cursor right keys.

To insert additional information into a file, simply position the cursor to an appropriate location and type the new information.

There are many more cursor control commands that move the cursor faster and easier.

| | |
|---|---|
| Escape, F | Moves the cursor ahead one word. |
| Escape, B | Moves the cursor back one word. |
| Control-A | Moves the cursor to the beginning of the current line. |
| Control-E | Moves the cursor to the end of the current line. |
| Escape, A | Moves the cursor to the beginning of the current sentence. |
| Escape, E | Moves the cursor to the end of the current sentence. |

| | |
|---|---|
| Escape, P | Moves the cursor to the beginning of the paragraph. |
| Escape, N | Moves the cursor to the end of the paragraph. |
| Escape,< | Moves the cursor to the beginning of the file. |
| Escape,> | Moves the cursor to the end of the file. |

**Deleting**

Deleting data from a file is more complicated than inserting data. The commands for deleting from a file are similar in form to the cursor control commands.

| | |
|---|---|
| DEL | The delete key causes the previous character to be erased. |
| Control-D | Causes the next character to be erased. |
| Escape, DEL | Causes the previous word to be erased. |
| Escape, D | Causes the next word to be erased. |
| Control-C | Causes the data from the cursor to the end of the line to be erased. |
| Escape, K | Causes the data from the cursor to the end of the sentence to be erased. |
| Escape, Control K | Causes the entire line of the file to be deleted. |
| Escape, H Control-W | Causes an entire paragraph to be deleted. |

To delete an entire section of a document, move the cursor to the beginning of the section to be deleted and press the ESC key followed by pressing the space bar. Then move the cursor to the end of the section to be deleted and press Control-W.

### Scrolling

When a document is too large to be displayed on the monitor, it is necessary to display only one screenful of information at a time. The method of displaying a document as a set of screens is called scrolling. The Control-V command is used to scroll forward, and Control-Z is used to scroll backward.

To make the transition between sections of the file easier to follow, the last two lines of the last screen are displayed at the top of the current screen. When scrolling backward, the process is reversed. The first two lines of the last screen appear at the bottom of the current screen.

### Inserting

If more than a few words are being added to a file, it is convenient to open the necessary space in the file before inserting the new data. Control-O is used to open a line of the file for inserting. When the inserting is complete, Escape, Control-O is used to close the gap.

When some of the contents of a file are deleted or inserted, the file may become disorganized. Escape, Q is used to correct this problem. When Escape, Q is executed, the paragraph that contains the cursor is reorganized.

An entire file can be inserted in another file by executing a Control-X,I command. When this command is executed, a prompt at the bottom of the display asks for the name of the file to be inserted into the current file. The entire file is inserted at the current position of the cursor.

A paragraph can be moved to another position, or repeated in another location. To specify the desired paragraph, move the cursor to the paragraph and execute the Escape, H command. If you want the paragraph to be moved, execute Control-W. If you want the paragraph to be copied, but remain intact, execute Escape, W. Finally, move the cursor to the position where the paragraph is to be inserted. Execute Control-Y to insert the paragraph in the new location.

A similar procedure is used to move or copy an entire section of the file. Move the cursor to the beginning of the desired section and press the ESC key followed by pressing the space bar. Move the cursor to the end of the section and execute Escape, W to copy the section. If the section is to be moved, execte Control-W instead. Proceed by moving the cursor to the position where the section is to be inserted, and execute Control-Y. Remember that Escape, W is used to copy a section of a file without destroying the original. The Control-W command deletes the original section when it is moved.

**Searching**

The Perfect Writer program has the ability to locate a set of characters throughout a file. A word, number, phrase, or set of characters can be found quickly by executing a search command. The search commands can also be used to replace a word, phrase, etc. with another word or phrase.

The command Control-S is used to search from the cursor location to the end of the file for a specified word or group of characters. When Control-S is executed, the following message is displayed at the bottom of the display:

Search Forward For <ESC> :_

In response to this prompt, enter the number, word, or phrase that you would like to locate. When the entry is complete, press the Escape key to begin the search.

The search moves the cursor to the space after the specified word. If the file does not contain a match, the message "Not Found" is displayed beneath the echo line, at the bottom of the page.

If a match is found, the next match can be found by pressing Control-S, Escape.

The reverse search function is similar to the forward search except for the fact that the search is conducted from the cursor location to the beginning of the file. Also, the cursor is positioned at the beginning of the match instead of the end. The reverse search command is Control-R.

The search command can also be used with a replace option. The search and replace command is Escape, R. When this command is executed, the following prompt appears below the echo line:

Replace <ESC>:

Enter the characters that you want to replace followed by the ESC key. The following prompt then appears:

with <ESC>:

Enter the new data, followed by the ESC key. The Perfect Writer program then performs the search and replace procedure. The search is always performed from the cursor position to the end of the file.

The search and replace command can also be used with an extended set of instructions. When the Escape, Control-R command is executed, the program waits for a response from the user each time a match is encountered.

Each time a match is encountered, the following prompt is displayed:

Replacing '*expression 1*' with '*expression 2*'

In the preceding prompt, *expression 1* and *expression 2* represent the old and new expressions in the file. These expressions are entered in response to the preceding prompts.

Each time the Replacing... prompt is displayed, the program waits for another command. There are six commands that can be used. These commands are summarized in Table 3-1.

**Table 3-1. Search and Replace Commands**

| | |
|---|---|
| Y | Make the replacement |
| N | Do not make the replacement |
| Period (.) | Quit searching and return the cursor to the original position. |
| Control-G | Quit searching and do not move the cursor from its current position. |
| Exclamation (!) | Perform the replacement for all subsequent matches. |
| Comma (,) | Make the replacement, but ask for confirmation (Y or N). |

**Utilities**

There are several miscellaneous commands that can also be used in the Perfect Writer program.

The Escape, S command causes the line that contains the cursor to be centered on the display.

The Control-G command is used to eliminate a preceding command. This command cannot compensate for all mistakes, but many problems can be avoided by using the back-up command.

The repeat command can be used to repeat any keystroke any number of times. This command consists of pressing the ESC key, followed by the number of repetitions desired. Whichever key follows the repeat command will be repeated the specified number of times. For example, the following keystrokes cause 20 asterisks (*) to be displayed:

ESC 20*

The quit command is used to exit a file without recording the modifications. Any changes that were made in a file before the quit command was executed will not actually change the file as it is recorded on the diskette. The quit command consists of the following keystrokes:

Control-X
Control-C

If a file is not modified in any way while it is in the edit mode, the quit command automatically returns the program to the menu.

However, if a file is edited before the quit command is executed, the quit command does not actually make the editions in the diskette file. In order to prevent modifications from being accidentally lost, the following prompt appears below the echo line when the quit command is executed for a modified file.

Abandon Modified Buffer(s)?

This prompt appears in order to make sure that the user actually wants to exit the file without making a copy of the modifications.

If the response to this prompt is Y, the program returns to the menu. If the response is N, the program remains in the edit mode.

Recall that the command,

Control-X
Control-S

is used to make a copy of a modified file on a diskette. When this command is executed, the old file on the diskette is replaced by the new file.

**Buffers**

The Perfect Writer program allows several files to be edited at the same time. This is achieved by manipulating buffers. A buffer is a section of the computer's memory that is used to edit a file. The word processor program can maintain up to 7 buffers.

The name of the buffer is generally the filename (without the drive specifier or the filename extension).

Table 3-2 contains the buffer name that is automatically assigned to several files.

**Table 3-2. Filenames and the Associated Buffer Name**

| Filename | Buffer Name |
|---|---|
| A:BILLS.DAT | bills |
| PROGRAM1.BAS | program1 |
| MEMO323 | memo323 |
| B:CHAPTER1.MMS | chapter1 |

A buffer name is assigned to a file unless the appropriate name is already assigned to a buffer. In this case, the following prompt is displayed below the echo line:

Buffer Exists! Buffer to Use <CR> :_

In this case, the buffer name is specified by the user, followed by pressing the Return key.

The important aspects of using multiple buffers are summarized as follows.

1. The file being edited is automatically assigned to a buffer.
2. Additional buffers are created by the command Control-X, Control-F.
3. Switch from buffer to buffer with the Control-X, B command.
4. Control-X, Control-B provides a list of active buffers.
5. Use Control-X, K to delete a buffer.

To begin using multiple buffers, simply edit a file as usual. The file being edited is automatically assigned to a buffer.

In order to access another file, execute the command Control-X, Control-F. The following prompt will appear at the bottom of the display:

File to Find <CR>:

Simply specify the other file that you wish to edit. New or existing files can be edited in this fashion. If the appropriate buffer already exists, you will be required to specify a new buffer name.

Switching from one file to another is achieved with the Control-X,B command. This command causes the following prompt to be displayed below the echo line:

Switch to Buffer <CR>:

In response, enter the desired buffer, followed by pressing the Return key.

Each buffer is edited in the same way that any file is edited. All the editor commands remain the same.

To obtain a list of the active buffers, execute the Control-X, Control-B command. An example of a buffer directory is provided in Illustration 3-1.

**Illustration 3-1. Example Buffer Directory**

| | | | |
|---|---|---|---|
| bills | 3027 | * | A:BILLS.DAT |
| program1 | 1015 | | PROGRAM1.BAS |
| memo323 | 2043 | | MEMO323 |
| chapter1 | 745 | * | B:CHAPTER.MMS |

The asterisks in Illustration 3-1 are used to designate that a file has been modified.

To delete a buffer, simply execute the command Control-X,K. The following prompt is displayed when the delete command is executed:

Delete Buffer <CR>:

In response to the prompt, enter the name of the buffer to be deleted, followed by the Return key.

### Modes

The word processor can operate in several modes. The most commonly used modes are Save, Fill, and Normal. In addition to these, View and Overwrite are also usable.

The Save mode is used to automatically record the file being edited after each 512 characters. This prevents a large amount of data from being lost if a problem occurs. Unfortunately, a lengthy document requires a considerable amount of time to be saved. As a result, the longer a document becomes, the more inconvenient the Save mode becomes.

The Fill mode is generally used to edit documents. This mode causes a line of the display to be filled with as many complete words as possible. In this mode, a word that exceeds the end of the line is automatically moved to the next line.

The Normal mode is generally used to edit computer programs. This mode is different from the Fill mode because the last word on the line is not automatically moved to the next line. At the end of the line, the display continues at the next line without preserving the words.

The View mode is used to review files without making any modifications. This is convenient to use when it is necessary for a file to remain unchanged.

The Overwrite mode is not commonly used. In this mode, the characters typed in a file are not inserted. Instead, the new characters take the place of the old ones, or overwrite them.

The default mode for the Perfect Writer program is the Fill mode. To change the mode, use the Control-X,M command. When this command is executed, the following prompt appears below the echo line.

Mode Name<CR>:

In response to this prompt, enter the name of the desired mode, followed by Return.

Since the Perfect Writer program can operate in more than one mode it is often necessary to cancel an undesired mode. The Control-X, Control-M command is used to delete a mode. Enter the name of the unwanted mode in response to the following prompt:

Delete Mode<CR>:

Press the Return key when the appropriate response is complete.

### Split Screen Editing

The Perfect Writer program allows two files to be edited at the same time. This procedure is called split-screen editing. This is achieved by dividing the display into two sections.

When two files are being edited at the same time, there is still only one cursor. As a result, the cursor must be moved to the appropriate section of the screen before the commands are executed.

The echo line at the bottom of the monitor displays the information about the file that contains the cursor.

To enter the split-screen edit mode, execute the following command:

Control-X,2

To return to the single screen mode, execute the following command:

Control-X,1

When the split screen edit mode is entered, the first part of the display is duplicated and separated by a horizontal line through the middle of the display. The cursor resides in the top half of the screen.

The procedure for obtaining the second file on the screen is exactly the same process that is used to create multiple buffers. When the Control-X, Control-F command is executed, the following prompt is displayed at the bottom of the display:

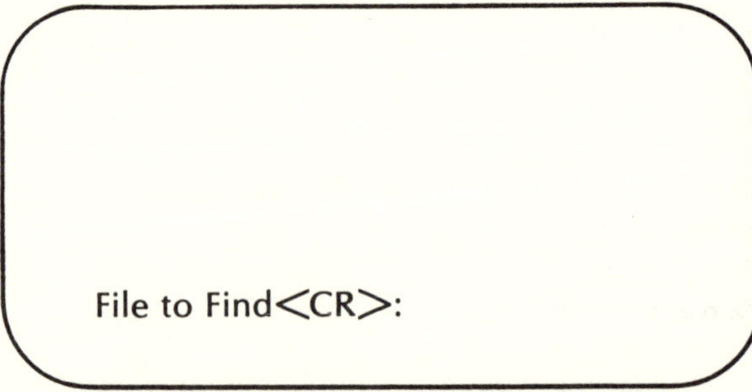

In response to this prompt, enter the name of the file that is to appear on the top half of the display. This file can now be edited with the usual commands.

There are also several commands that make split screen editing much easier. These commands are summarized in Table 3-3.

**Table 3-3. Split-Screen Editing Commands**

| | |
|---|---|
| Control-X,^ | Enlarge the current screen. |
| Control-Z | Scroll the current screen backward. |
| Control-V | Scroll the current screen forward. |
| Control-X,O | Move the cursor to the other screen. |
| Control-X, Control-Z | Scroll the other screen backward. |
| Control-X, Control-V | Scroll the other screen forward. |

To enlarge the part of the screen that contains the cursor, execute the Control-X,^ command. Note that the carat (∧) is the shift-6 character on the keyboard. This command only moves the boundary one line. To enlarge the area by several lines, use the repeat function. For example, the command,

Escape,6, Control-X,^

would enlarge the part of the display that contains the cursor by 6 lines.

Generally, the editing commands are only effective for the part of the display that contains the cursor. The only commands that affect the other screen are the following:

Control-X, Control-Z
Control-X, Control-V

These commands are used to scroll the "other" screen.

To move the cursor from one section of the display, execute the Control-X,O command. In effect, this command switches the "current" and "other" screen.

## FORMAT COMMANDS

The commands of the preceding section were used to manipulate the editing features of the Perfect Writer program. The rest of this chapter contains a description of the commands used to design a document. These commands are actually placed in the text of a file to control the format of the final output document.

The three main types of document design commands are environment, typeface, and organization.

Environment commands are used to control the way that the text appears in the file. The typeface commands control the type of characters that are used to print the text. The organization commands are used to arrange the text within the file.

The "at sign" (@) is used to indicate that the following word is a format command. All of the commands must be preceded by an at sign.

The section of the text that is affected by the command must be set off from the rest of the text. This is achieved by the use of **fences.** A fence is a character that is used to separate a section of text from the body of the document. Generally, parentheses are used as the fences, but several other characters can also be used (see Table 3-4).

**Table 3-4. Fences for Format Commands**

| | |
|---|---|
| ( ) | parentheses |
| < > | angle brackets |
| " " | double quotes |
| ' ' | single quotes |
| [ ] | square brackets |
| { } | braces |

The following command is an example of the correct format for a document design command.

@ CENTER (FORMATS OF DOCUMENT DESIGN COMMANDS)

The preceding command causes the text enclosed in parentheses to be centered on the page. The word @CENTER does not appear in the final copy of the output even though it appears in the file. Similarly, the parentheses do not appear in the output.

Commands that are used over a large section of the text can also use the @BEGIN/@END format. The following example has the same results as the preceding example.

@BEGIN(CENTER) FORMATS OF DOCUMENT DESIGN
COMMANDS @END(CENTER)

If the commands are used within other commands, be sure to use the @BEGIN/@END technique to avoid confusion, or simply use a different type of fence for each command.

Examples in this section have the following format.

XXXXXXXXXXXXXXXXXXXXX

1. Examples are enclosed in a border.
2. The text in standard type represents the effect of the command.
3. XXXX... represents the text that is not affected by the command.

XXXXXXXXXXXXXXXXXXXX

**ADDRESS**

The ADDRESS command is used to position an address in the center of a page.

**Example**

@ADDRESS (WILLIAM JONES
3847 NEWBERG AVE.
SOUTH EUCLID, OH 44159)

WILLIAM JONES
3847 NEWBERG AVE.
SOUTH EUCLID, OH 44159

XXXXXXXXXX
XXXXXXXXXXXXXXXXXXXX
XXXXXXXXXX

**CENTER**

The CENTER command is used to print one or several lines of output in the center of the line of output.

**Example**

@CENTER (PERFECT WRITER
BY PERFECT SOFTWARE INC.)

```
XXXXXXXXXXXXXXXXXXXXXXXXXXXXXXXX

         PERFECT WRITER
  BY PERFECT SOFTWARE, INC.

XXXXXXXXXXXXXXXXXXXXXXXXXXXXXXXX
```

The CENTER command automatically provides a blank line between the body of the text and the section that is centered.

**CLOSING**

The CLOSING command is used to put one or several closing lines at the end of a letter. The closing is automatically aligned with the address at the top of the page.

**Example**

@CLOSING (Sincerely,
Tom Cash)

```
XXXXXXXXXXXXXXXXXXXXXXXXXXXX

                Sincerely,
                Tom Cash
```

The CLOSING command automatically inserts one blank line between the body of the text and the closing.

## DESCRIPTION

The DESCRIPTION command is generally used to provide definitions for terms.

**Example**

```
@BEGIN(DESCRIPTION)
CPU@/Central Processing Unit. This is the
electronic component that actually performs the
computer's calculations.

RAM@/Random Access Memory. This is the part
of the computer that is used to store programs or
data.
@END(DESCRIPTION)
```

XXXXXXXXXXXXXXXXXXXX

| | |
|---|---|
| CPU | Central Processing Unit. This is the electronic component that actually performs the computer's calculations. |
| RAM | Random Access Memory. This is the part of the computer that is used to store programs or data. |

XXXXXXXXXXXXXXXXXXXX

The DESCRIPTION command automatically provides a blank line between the definitions and the body of the text. However, blank lines must be provided between the definitions.

The characters @/ are used to establish the tab spacing between the terms and definitions. The definitions are single spaced and both left and right justified.

## DISPLAY

The DISPLAY command is used to insert text that has narrower margins than the body of the text.

**Example**

@DISPLAY(The most important thing to remember is
to turn the computer on before using it.)

XXXXXXXXXXXXXXXXXXXXXXXXXXXXXXXXXXX

The most important thing to remember is
to turn on the computer before using it.

XXXXXXXXXXXXXXXXXXXXXXXXXXXXXXXXXXX

The DISPLAY command does not manipulate the text in any way. Each line of the output corresponds exactly to the line of data in the file.

## ENUMERATE

The ENUMERATE command is used to number a set of topics.

**Example**

@ENUMERATE(MONITOR

KEYBOARD

DISK DRIVES

PRINTER)

XXXXXXXXXXXXXXX

1. MONITOR

2. KEYBOARD

3. DISK DRIVES

4. PRINTER

XXXXXXXXXXXXXXX

**FLUSHLEFT**

The FLUSHLEFT command is used to print the output so that every line is against the left margin. The text is not altered in any way, so the output appears exactly like the text in the file.

**Example**

```
@FLUSHLEFT(The Kaypro computer
is a product of:
Non-Linear Systems, Inc.)
```

XXXXXXXXXXXXXXXXXXXXXXXXXXXXXX

The Kaypro computer
is a product of:
Non-Linear Systems, Inc.

XXXXXXXXXXXXXXXXXXXXXXXXXXXXXX

**FLUSHRIGHT**

The FLUSHRIGHT command is used to print the output so that every line is against the right margin. This command does not alter the text in any way. Each line is merely moved to the right margin.

**Example**

@FLUSHRIGHT(The Kaypro computer
is a product of:
Non-Linear Systems, Inc.

```
xxxxxxxxxxxxxxxxxxxxxxxxxxxxxxxxxxxxxxx

                        The Kaypro computer
                            is a product of:
                   Non-Linear Systems, Inc.

xxxxxxxxxxxxxxxxxxxxxxxxxxxxxxxxxxxxxxx
```

## INDENT

The INDENT command is used to indent a section of the text. The right margin is the same for the entire text, only the left margin is indented.

In the indent mode, the text is manipulated in order to fit as many words as possible on each line.

**Example**

@INDENT (The Kaypro computer
is a product of
Non-Linear Systems, Inc.)

```
xxxxxxxxxxxxxxxxxxxxxxxxxxxxxxxxxxxxxxxxxxxxx

   The Kaypro computer is a product of Non-Linear
   Systems, Inc.

xxxxxxxxxxxxxxxxxxxxxxxxxxxxxxxxxxxxxxxxxxxxx
```

## ITEMIZE

The ITEMIZE command is used to list a set of topics. Each entry in the ITEMIZE command is preceded by a dash.

If a second ITEMIZE command is executed while the first command is in effect, each entry is preceded by an asterisk.

**Example**

@ITEMIZE(MONITOR

KEYBOARD

DISK DRIVES

PRINTER)

```
XXXXXXXXXXXXXXXXXXXX

-  MONITOR

-  KEYBOARD

-  DISK DRIVES

-  PRINTER

XXXXXXXXXXXXXXXXXXXX
```

## LEVEL

The LEVEL command is used to number and indent paragraphs of any other items. If a LEVEL command is executed while another LEVEL command is in effect, the second level is indented further. Each additional level has the number of the preceding item plus an additional number.

**Example**

```
@LEVEL(MONITOR

KEYBOARD

DISK DRIVES   @LEVEL {DRIVE A

DRIVE B}

PRINTER)
```

```
XXXXXXXXXXXXXXXXXXXXXXXXXXXXXXXXXXXX

      1.  MONITOR

      2.  KEYBOARD

      3.  DISK DRIVES

          3.1. DRIVE A
          3.2. DRIVE B

      4.  PRINTER

XXXXXXXXXXXXXXXXXXXXXXXXXXXXXXXXXXXX
```

## QUOTATION

The QUOTATION command is used to indent the right and left margins of a section of text. The text is manipulated to include as many words as possible on a line of output.

**Example**

```
@QUOTATION(Breakthroughs in integrated
circuit technology have made the microcomputer
a reality. The current technology allows micro-
processors to be combined with random access
memory to achieve an inexpensive computer
system.)
```

```
XXXXXXXXXXXXXXXXXXXXXXXXXXXXXXXXXXXXXXX

Breakthroughs in integrated circuit technology have
made the microcomputer a reality. The current
technology allows microprocessors to be combined with
random access memory to achieve an inexpensive computer
system.

XXXXXXXXXXXXXXXXXXXXXXXXXXXXXXXXXXXXXXX
```

**TEXT**

The TEXT command is used to manipulate the contents of a file to fill all the lines and justify both margins. Also, each new paragraph is properly indented.

**Example**

```
@BEGIN(TEXT)
The dual disk drives built into
the Kaypro computer provide
a fast, accurate, and        inexpensive
                 way to record data and
programs.
@END(TEXT)
```

```
XXXXXXXXXXXXXXXXXXXXXXXXXXXXXXXXXXX

     The dual disk drives built into the Kaypro
computer provide a fast, accurate, and inexpensive
way to record data and programs.

XXXXXXXXXXXXXXXXXXXXXXXXXXXXXXXXXXX
```

## UNDENT

The UNDENT command is used to extend the first line of each paragraph into the left margin.

**Example**

@BEGIN(UNDENT)

The dual disk drives built into the Kaypro computer provide a fast, accurate, and inexpensive way to record programs and data.

The numeric keypad allows numeric data to be entered quickly and easily.

@END(UNDENT)

XXXXXXXXXXXXXXXXXXXXXXXXXX

The dual disk drives built into the Kaypro computer provide a fast, accurate, and inexpensive way to record programs and data.

The numeric keypad allows numeric data to be entered quickly and easily.

XXXXXXXXXXXXXXXXXXXXXXXXXX

## VERBATIM

The VERBATIM command is used to produce output that appears exactly like the data in the file.

**Example**

```
@BEGIN(VERBATIM)
         ITEM      QTY.     PRICE

         pens      2000     $.15
        pencils    1500     $.05

@END(VERBATIM)
```

```
XXXXXXXXXXXXXXXXXXXXXXXXX

              ITEM        QTY.     PRICE

              pens        2000     $.15
              pencils     1500     $.05

XXXXXXXXXXXXXXXXXXXXXXXXX
```

## VERSE

The VERSE command is used to output data that is meant to be presented as lines of data. Each line of a verse is presented in its original form unless it is too long to fit on one line. Each line that is too long is continued on the next line and indented.

**Example**

```
@BEGIN(VERSE)
Keyboard
Numeric keypad
Dual mini-floppy double-density soft sectored disk drives
Monitor
@END(VERSE)
```

```
XXXXXXXXXXXXXXXXXXXXXXXXXXXXXX

      Keyboard
      Numeric keypad
      Dual mini-floppy double-density soft sectored
          disk drives
      Monitor

XXXXXXXXXXXXXXXXXXXXXXXXXXXXXX
```

## PRINT STYLES

The type of printer used with the Kaypro computer determines the types of characters that can be printed. If the printer cannot print in different type faces, the typeface commands have no effect. Table 3-5 contains a summary of the typeface commands.

**Table 3-5. Typeface Commands**

| Command | Style |
|---|---|
| @B | Boldface type |
| @I | Italics |
| @P | Boldface italics |
| @R | Roman type |
| @T | Typewriter style |
| @U | Underline all characters |
| @UN | Underline characters A through Z |
| @UX | Underline all characters and spaces |
| @+ | Superscript |
| @– | Subscript |

Be sure to enclose the section of text in a set of fences. The format of these commands is the same as the environment commands.

**Example**

@B { This is an example of @I(two different type styles) used at the same time}

XXXXXXXXXXXXXXXXXXXXXXXXX

**This is an example of** *two different type styles* **used at the same time.**

XXXXXXXXXXXXXXXXXXXXXXXXX

## ORGANIZATION

The organizational commands are used with the Perfect Writer program in order to set up the headings of a document.

The headings can be either numbered or unnumbered. When numbered headings are used, a table of contents is automatically generated for the document.

The organizational commands can also be used to make footnotes as well as an index. Page headings can also be generated with these commands.

The four unnumbered heading commands are summarized in Table 3-6.

**Table 3-6. Unnumbered Heading Commands**

| Command | Typeface | Preceding Lines | Following Lines | Position | New Page |
|---|---|---|---|---|---|
| @UNNUMBERED | Bold | 6 | 2 | Center | Yes |
| @MAJORHEADING | Bold | 6 | 2 | Center | No |
| @HEADING | Bold | 4 | 2 | Center | No |
| @SUBHEADING | Underline | 4 | 2 | Left | No |

The numbered headings are used to label the sections of a document and generate a table of contents as well. Unlike the unnumbered headings, the numbered headings are always preceded by an appropriate number. The following example displays the format of a typical subsection.

**Example**

1.3.2 CP/M COMMANDS

This example demonstrates the format of a numbered heading. The subsection (CP/M COMMANDS) is the second subsection within the third section of the first chapter.

Table 3-7 includes a summary of the six numbered heading commands.

**Table 3-7. Numbered Heading Commands**

| Command | Type | Preceding Lines | Following Lines | Position | New Page |
|---|---|---|---|---|---|
| @CHAPTER | Bold | 6 | 3 | Center | Yes |
| @SECTION | Underline | 4 | 2 | Left | No |
| @SUBSECTION | Standard | 2 | 1 | Left | No |
| @PARAGRAPH | Standard | 2 | 1 | Left | No |
| @APPENDIX | Bold | 6 | 3 | Center | Yes |
| @APPENDIXSECTION | Underline | 4 | 2 | Left | No |

The table of contents is organized according to the numbered headings, the page numbers are also listed in the table of contents. Illustration 3-1 contains a typical table of contents which is generated by using numbered headings.

**Illustration 3-1. A Typical Table of Contents**

Table of Contents



An index can also be generated for a document by using the index command. The format of the index command is as follows:

@INDEX(*topic*)

Whenever an INDEX command is encountered in the body of a file, an entry into the index is made under the specified *topic*. The INDEX statement and *topic* do not actually appear in the output text, only in the output index. Illustration 3-2 contains an example of an index.

**Illustration 3-2. A Typical Index**

Index

AMPERE 21
AMPLIFIER, CURRENT 22
AMPLIFIER, VOLTAGE 24
AMPLITUDE 4
ANALOG 6
ANODE 85
AUTOMATIC GAIN CONTROL 57
BANDPASS 37
BANDWIDTH 39
BIAS, CURRENT 29
BIAS, VOLTAGE 28
BISTABLE MULTIVIBRATOR 60

Footnotes can be generated with the FOOT command. The footnotes appear at the bottom of the page, and are automatically numbered.

A footnote has the following format:

@FOOT(*footnote*)

The parameter *footnote* represents the actual text of the footnote.

End notes, or "footnotes", collected at the end of a document are generated in a similar fashion to footnotes. The following format is used to create end notes:

@NOTE(*end note*)

Pageheadings and pagefootings can also be generated with the Perfect Writer program. The PAGEHEADING command is used to print a label at the top of each page of a document. Each label can have a left, center, and right portion. If any portion of a pageheading is not assigned a value, it automatically is blank.

The following format is used to assign a pageheading for a document:

@PAGEHEADING(LEFT = "*leftheading*", CENTER = "*centerheading*", RIGHT = "*rightheading*")

The italicized values represent the actual pageheadings that appear on each page of a document.

The PAGEFOOTING command has exactly the same format as the PAGEHEADING command. However, if no PAGEFOOTING is specified, the pages are automatically numbered sequentially.

**Variables**

The VALUE and STRING commands are used by the Perfect Writer program to assign values to string variables. A string variable is a name that represents a set of characters. If the variable is assigned a new value, the variable name will represent the new value. The STRING command is used to assign a value to a variable. The VALUE command is used to recover the value that the variable represents.

For example, a person's name may be repeated throughout a letter. It would be difficult and time consuming to edit a letter so that each name entry was edited individually. To solve this problem, variables are used with the Perfect Writer program.

**Example**

```
@STRING(NAME = "TOM CASH")
HELLO @VALUE(NAME)!
```

The preceding example contains a demonstration of the use of the STRING and VALUE commands.

In the first line, the value TOM CASH is assigned to the variable NAME. In the second line, the VALUE command is used to return the value of the variable NAME. When the example file is formatted, the final output is as follows:

HELLO TOM CASH!

The CASE command is used to choose a particular section of the file for the output. For instance, if a letter has a different opening paragraph for different times of the year, the appropriate selection can be made with a CASE statement.

A CASE statement uses a control variable to choose a selection. Consider the following example CASE statement.

@CASE { season,

spring,"Start preparing your car now for the difficult summer months ahead."

summer,"The summer months are miserable for your car."

fall,"Start preparing your car now for the difficult winter months ahead."

winter,"The winter months can get the best of your car." }

The control variable in this example is "season". This is the first value specified in the CASE command.

The four paragraphs that follow the control variable are four possible opening lines of a letter. Notice that each paragraph begins with a word followed by a comma. This word designates the paragraph. When the control variable is assigned this value, the paragraph that starts with that value is included in the final output.

The control variable is assigned a value with a STRING statement. An appropriate STRING command is as follows:

@STRING(season = "fall")

The STRING command must precede the CASE command. Since the control variable, season, is assigned the value "fall", only the third paragraph in the selection is actually included in the final output of the file.

There are a set of variables that are automatically assigned values. These values are the names of the current chapter, section, subsection, etc. The VALUE command is used with these variables to generate the headings of a document. These variables are generally used in page headings or footings. The following list contains the heading variables.

CHAPTERTITLE
SECTIONTITLE
SUBSECTIONTITLE
PARAGRAPHTITLE
APPENDIXTITLE
APPENDIXSECTIONTITLE

In addition to the heading variables, Perfect Writer also contains a set of counter variables. The counters keep track of the number of pages, chapter, sections, etc. in a document.

The set of counters used with the Perfect Writer program have the following names:

PAGE
CHAPTER
SECTION
SUBSECTION
PARAGRAPH
APPENDIX
APPENDIXSECTION

The SET and REF commands are used to make correct references to a previous part of a document. For instance, if a discussion of transistors is noteworthy in a document, the page (or chapter, etc.) can be assigned to a variable and referenced later. The use of SET and REF prevent problems that would occur with referencing if pages, sections, or chapters were inserted or deleted from the document.

**Example**

...The invention of the transistor @SET(TRANS = page)
was probably the most important...

...As discussed on page @REF(TRANS), the transistor
became...

In the preceding example, the first section of the document contains an important discussion that is referenced later in the document. A SET command is used to assign the page number to the variable TRANS.

A REF command can be used later in the document to return the value of the variable TRANS. In this section of the file, the page number of the SET command will be returned.

**NEWPAGE, BLANKPAGE, BLANKSPACE**

The command that is used to proceed to a new page is called NEWPAGE. The command that is used to leave an entire blank page in a document is the BLANKPAGE command. The BLANKPAGE command requires a number following the command in order to specify the number of blank pages.

**Example**

@BLANKPAGE(2)

The BLANKSPACE command is used to insert blank lines in a document. The number of blank lines must be specified along with the word "lines".

**Example**

@BLANKSPACE(5 LINES)

### MESSAGE & INCLUDE

The MESSAGE command is used to display a prompt on the display while a file is being formatted. This command is generally used along with the INCLUDE command. INCLUDE is used to insert another file, or data from the keyboard into the file being formatted.

**Example**

@INCLUDE(PARTII.MMS)

The previous example contains a command that is used to insert the file PARTII.MMS into the file being formatted. If this file does not exist on the specified diskette, an error will occur when the file is formatted.

The INCLUDE command can also be used to insert data into the file from the keyboard.

**Example**

@INCLUDE(CON:)

The previous example contains a command that is used to enter data from the keyboard. (CON: is the device name used in CP/M for the keyboard.)

When the final data has been entered from the keyboard, execute the following command to continue formatting of the file.

Control-Z

## COMMENTS

The COMMENT command is used to insert information into the file to explain the contents of the file. The COMMENT command has no effect on the output.

**Example**

@COMMENT(Be sure that this is the last chapter)

## STYLE

The STYLE command is used to change any of the parameters that are used by the Perfect Writer program. A summary of the STYLE command is supplied in Table 3-8.

**Table 3-8. STYLE Command Parameters**

| Parameter | Explanation | Format/Default Value |
|---|---|---|
| ABOVE | Blank lines preceding format options. | (ABOVE 1 LINE) |
| BELOW | Blank lines following format options. | (BELOW 1 LINE) |
| BOTTOMMARGIN | Blank lines at bottom of page. | (BOTTOMMARGIN 3 LINES) |
| CHAPTERS | Number chapters and appendices. | (CHAPTERS YES) |
| FOOTERSPACING | Lines between text and page footings. | FOOTERSPACING 3 LINES) |
| FOOTPUSH | Footnote numbers Yes: superscript<br>No: square bracket | (FOOTPUSH YES) |
| HEADERSPACING | Lines between text and page heading | (HEADERSPACING 3 LINES) |
| INDENT | Spaces indented or undented | (INDENT 2 CHARS) |

| Parameter | Explanation | Format/Default Value |
|---|---|---|
| JUSTIFICATION | Right justification | (JUSTIFICATION YES) |
| LEFTMARGIN | Left margin | (LEFTMARGIN 8 CHARS) |
| LEVELHANG | Undent numbers in LEVEL mode | (LEVELHANG NO) |
| LEVELINDENT | Indent nested LEVEL paragraphs | (LEVELINDENT YES) |
| LINEWIDTH | Number of characters per line | (LINEWIDTH 60 CHARS)* |
| NOTES | Footnote location: bottom, endnote, inline. | (NOTES BOTTOM) |
| PAPERLENGTH | Paper length | (PAPERLENGTH 11 INCHES) |
| PAPERWIDTH | Paper width | (PAPERWIDTH 9 INCHES) |
| RIGHTMARGIN | Right margin | (RIGHTMARGIN 8 CHARS) |
| SCRIPTPUSH | Compensate spacing for superscript, subscript. | (SCRIPTPUSH YES) |
| SPACING | Spaces for each line of output | (SPACING 1 LINE) |
| SPREAD | Lines between paragraphs | (SPREAD 1 LINE) |
| TOPMARGIN | Blank lines above page header | (TOPMARGIN 3 LINES) |

* No Default Value

When the STYLE commands are used with a document, they must be the first commands in the file.

**Examples**

@STYLE(PAPERWIDTH 12 INCHES)
@STYLE(INDENT 8 SPACES)

A STYLE command is used when the default values of a parameter are not suitable for a particular use. For example, if you wish to use paper that is 12 inches wide, use the PAPERWIDTH command to specify the new paper width. The use of the STYLE command for paper width is demonstrated in the preceding example.

The default value for indentation of paragraphs is 2 spaces. If you would prefer a larger indentation, use the INDENT command to specify a new value. This command is also demonstrated in the preceding example.

If no STYLE commands are included in a file, each parameter is automatically assigned the default value as listed in Table 3-8.

## FORMATTING AND PRINTING FILES

Once a file has been created and stored on a diskette, the file is ready to be formatted. Formatting is the process whereby all the format commands are executed.

When the editing of a file is complete, execute the following command to save the file on a diskette.

Control-X
Control-S

Unless the filename includes a drive specifier (A: or B:), the file will be saved on the diskette in the default drive. Recall that the default drive is the drive name that appears in the system prompt (A> or B>).

When using the Perfect Writer program, insert a blank, formatted diskette in drive B, and specify drive B in the filename.

When the file has been saved on the diskette, execute the following command to return to the Perfect Writer menu:

Control-X
Control-C

If the filename that contains the document does not have a filename extension of MMS, choose selection R from the menu to change the name of the file. The format program will not execute unless the filename extension is MMS.

Once the file has been successfully renamed, the format procedure will be ready to begin. Choose selection F from the menu and respond to the next prompt with the filename that contains the document.

**Quick Print**

When the Format selection is chosen, another menu will be displayed on the monitor. To print the finished document on the printer, choose selection P. To view the finished copy on the monitor, choose selection C. Both of these choices ( C or P) require that G also be selected from the menu. When G is selected, the file will be formatted and displayed (or printed). The use of this "quick print" option does not allow the use of different type faces.

**Full Feature Print**

The full feature print allows several options that the quick print option does not. These include different type faces, multiple copies of documents, and the ability to print only a part of a document.

To perform a full feature print, choose selection O (Name the output file differently) from the format menu (instead of C or P). When this selection is chosen, the following prompt appears at the bottom of the screen:

What do you wish to name the output file?

The filename specified in response to this prompt automatically is assigned the filename extension .FIN. After the output filename is specified, press G in order to start the format procedure.

When the formatting is complete, the original Perfect Writer menu is displayed. Choose selection P (Print a formatted file) to output the formatted file on the printer. When this selection is chosen, the name of the formatted file must be specified.

The Perfect Writer Printer Selection Menu appears on the display after the formatted filename is specified. Generally, only selection G is required from this menu.

A prompt appears at the bottom of the display that specifies the filename and device name of the printer. Press the Y key in order to print the formatted file on the printer.

# CHAPTER 4.
# PERFECT SPELLER

## INTRODUCTION

The Perfect Speller program is used to check the spelling of a document file. The Perfect Speller is used in conjunction with the Perfect Writer word processor.

The Perfect Speller program is very easy to use. The speller checks about 4000 words per minute using a "dictionary" that contains more than 50,000 words.

### Preparing a Diskette

The Perfect Speller master diskette is provided in the standard software package with the Kaypro computer. In order to make a working copy of the master diskette, perform the FORMAT, COPY and SYSGEN procedures as described in Chapter 2. Remember that the FORMAT command erases the contents of a diskette, so be sure to use a blank diskette or one that is no longer needed.

When the SYSGEN command has been executed, a copy of the operating system is recorded on the diskette. This allows the working copy to be used to "start up" the computer. The master diskette is "write protected" and does not contain a copy of CP/M. As a result, the master Perfect Speller diskette generally cannot be used. The set of master diskettes are not intended for everyday use. The masters are intended to be copied and placed in a safe area.

## Getting Started

The Perfect Speller program is used to check the spelling of a file that is created with the Perfect Writer program. The Perfect Speller diskette contains the Perfect Writer programs as well as the Perfect Speller programs.

As a result, the Speller diskette can be used to create and edit files, as well as check the spelling of the files.

When the computer is powered on, the following prompt appears on the display:

```
          * KAYPRO II *

Please insert your diskette in drive A
```

In response to this prompt, insert a working copy of the Perfect Speller diskette in drive A. When the drive door is closed, the following message should appear on the screen:

```
KAYPRO II
64k CP/M v 2.2

A>
```

If a different message appears on the display, the diskette probably does not have a copy of the operating system.

When the system prompt (A>) appears on the display, enter the MENU command, followed by pressing the Return key.

A>MENU

In response to this command, the Perfect Writer menu is diplayed. From this menu, files are created and edited with the usual Perfect Writer format.

It is generally an excellent idea to store the document files on a diskette in drive B. When a blank, formatted diskette is present in the lower drive, the file name drive specifier B: is used to designate drive B. For example, all of the following files would be stored on the diskette in drive B.

B:CHAPTER.MMS
B:MEMO.MMS
B:PROGRAM1.BAS

If a filename specifier is not included in a filename, the file is automatically created on the diskette in the default drive. The default drive is the drive that appears in the system prompt (A> or B>). The system prompt can be changed by entering the new default drive followed by a colon.

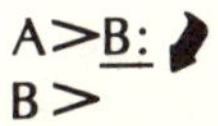

A>B:
B>

The default drive can only be chosen before the menu is displayed. However, when drive B is the default drive, the drive specifier A: must be used with the MENU command (A:MENU).

Chapter 3 contains a complete explanation of the usage of the Perfect Writer program to create and edit files. The sample file used in this chapter (B: THANKS) can be created and saved on a blank diskette in drive B using the procedure on pages 50 to 53.

The file B: THANKS has the following contents:

> Dear Grandma,
> Thank you very much for the birthday gift.
> Sincerely,

**Concept**

The general operation of the Perfect Speller program consists of two procedures. The first step in using the program to edit a file is to scan the list of unrecognized words. Even though the program can recognize more than 50,000 words, there are some words that can be correctly spelled, but still not recognized.

As a result, it is convenient to scan the list of unrecognized words to eliminate the words that do not need to be corrected. This step makes the editing procedure much easier.

Once the unrecognized words have been eliminated, the remaining problem words are marked within the file. When the program returns to the edit mode, the spelling of the marked words in the file can be corrected.

When all the corrections have been made, the process should be repeated to be sure that some of the "corrections" are not incorrect.

**Procedure**

Suppose the example was typed incorrectly so the following information is saved in the disk file.

> Dear Grandma,
> Think yoo very much forr the birthday gift.
> Sincerelie,

Notice that this file has the words *you, for* and *sincerely* misspelled. Also, the word *think* has been placed in the file instead of *thank*. Although the program can locate words that are not spelled correctly, the program has no way of knowing that the word *think* is supposed to be *thank*.

As a result, the Perfect Speller program cannot be used to correct such errors. If the wrong word is used in a file, or the file contains a grammatical error, the Perfect Writer word processor must be used to correct the error.

When the Perfect Writer is in the edit mode, the Perfect Speller programs are activated by the following command.

Control-X,S

This command is executed by holding down the CTRL key while typing "X", followed by typing "S" (after releasing the CTRL key).

When this command is executed, the following prompt appears at the bottom of the display:

File to Spell <CR>:

In response to this prompt, type the name of the file that contains the document that needs its spelling checked. For the example, enter B:THANKS, followed by pressing the Return key.

File to Spell <CR> :B:THANKS ↵

After the file name has been entered, the following messages will be displayed at the bottom of the display.

PERFECT SPELLER 1.1 (c) 1982 Perfect Software, Inc.
11 words processed. 3 words not recognized. Scan list of unrecognized words now <Yes>?

## Scanning

If the response to the Scan list prompt is yes, each word that does not match an entry in the Perfect Speller "dictionary" will be displayed at the bottom of the monitor. When each unrecognized word is displayed, one of the commands A,C,E,I,R or ? can be entered. The effect of each of these commands is summarized in Table 4-1.

**Table 4-1. Perfect Speller Commands**

| Command | Operation |
|---|---|
| A | Add the unrecognized word to the dictionary |
| C | Change the spelling of the unrecognized word. |
| E | Quit scanning and switch to the edit mode. |
| I | Ignore the unrecognized word. |
| R | Add the root of the unrecognized word to the dictionary. |
| ? | Display the set of available commands. |

If the word that is unrecognized is in fact properly spelled, choose command A to add the correct spelling of the word into the dictionary.

If the unrecognized word is correctly spelled, but it is a word with a suffix and/or prefix (i.e. disenchanted) use the R command and enter only the root of the word (ie. enchant) into the dictionary. This allows many forms of the new word to be recognized instead of only one form.

If an unrecognized word is correctly spelled, but is rarely used, use the I command to ignore the unrecognized word.

Use the C command to indicate that the spelling of a word actually needs to be changed.

Use the E command to quit scanning the unrecognized words and return to the edit mode. When this selection is chosen, the rest of the unrecognized words in the file are preceded by the characters ∿↑S.

If the response to the "Scan list" prompt was N, each unrecognized word in the file will be preceded with the characters ∿↑S. While this procedure is being performed, the following message is displayed.

```
Marking misspelled words in B: THANKS...
```

When the Scan list option is complete, the following prompt will be displayed at the bottom of the display.

```
Exit directly to PW <Yes>?
```

If the response to this prompt is no, the Perfect Writer menu is displayed on the monitor.

If the response to the prompt is yes, the Perfect Writer program returns to the edit mode for the specified file.

**Editing**

When the edit mode resumes, the cursor will be located at the first unrecognized word. Any subsequent unrecognized words have the ∿↑S characters preceding the word.

Each misspelled word will be displayed at the bottom of the monitor, followed by a colon. The same commands (see Table 4-1) are used again to actually correct the errors in the file.

The commands generally have the same effect in the edit mode as they do in the "Scan list" mode. However, the change command (C) actually allows the changes in spelling to be made. When the commands have been executed in the edit mode, the program will automatically proceed to the next unrecognized word.

**Perfect Speller Menu**

Instead of using the Control-X,S command to invoke the Perfect Speller programs, the speller can alternatively be accessed from the Perfect Writer Selection Menu. The Perfect Writer menu is the list of options that appear on the monitor when the MENU command is executed.

The prompt at the bottom of the menu appears as follows:

```
Type one character to indicate your selection now.
Your pleasure: (E,F,P,S,D,Z,R,C,X)
```

Choose selection S to check the spelling of a file. Another prompt then appears on the bottom of the screen.

```
Type the name of the file whose spelling you wish to check.
>
```

In response to the prompt, enter the file name, followed by the Return key.

When the file name has been entered, the Perfect Speller Selection Menu is displayed on the monitor. A brief explanation of each selection is included in Table 4-2.

**Table 4-2. Perfect Speller Selection Menu Options**

| | |
|---|---|
| A | Create an additional dictionary. |
| B | Give the backup file the specified extension instead of .BAK. |
| D | Check the file with the specified dictionary instead of DICTIONARY.SPL |
| L | List the unrecognized words in the file on the monitor. |
| M | Mark the unrecognized words with the specified character instead of ~↑S. |
| N | Do not make a backup file. |
| O | Send the results of the program to a specified disk file. |
| P | Use a specific table of prefixes and suffixes. |
| G | Begin the spelling check procedure. |
| X | Return to the Perfect Writer Selection Menu. |

The operation of the Perfect Speller program will basically be the same regardless of the procedure used to activate the program.

When the speller is selected from the Perfect Writer menu, a backup file will automatically be generated. The backup file has the same filename as the original file except for the filename extension. A backup file is assigned the filename extension .BAK. The filename extension of the backup file can be changed with selection B from the Perfect Speller Selection Menu.

## Dictionaries

Several additional dictionaries are available from Perfect Software, Inc. for specific spelling needs. These include medical, legal, and foreign language dictionaries, as well as many others.

Generally, the standard dictionary (DICTIONARY.SPL) is acceptable for a wide range of applications. Additional entries can be added to the standard dictionary to make the Perfect Speller program even more versatile.

Words can be entered into the dictionary in one of three ways. The first method is to add the word to the dictionary with the A command while scanning a list of unrecognized words.

The second method is to use the R command to enter the root of a compound word into the dictionary. Entering the root of a word allows many forms of the word to be recognized.

The Perfect Speller program also has provisions for generating new dictionaries or making major revisions to the standard dictionary. These procedures are not difficult, but may become tedious. Although the standard dictionary is adequate for a wide range of applications, consult the **Perfect Speller User's Guide** for the procedure used to generate new dictionaries.

# CHAPTER 5.
# PERFECT FILER

---

## INTRODUCTION

The Perfect Filer program is used to maintain a record keeping system. This program has provisions to address mailing labels, to create form letters and to provide lists of the entries in the file according to name, address, city, etc.

The Perfect Filer program is useful for general record keeping as well as particular correspondence needs.

### Getting Started

The Perfect Filer master diskette is provided in the standard software package with the Kaypro computer. In order to make a working copy of the master diskette, perform the FORMAT, COPY and SYSGEN procedures as described in Chapter 2. Remember that the FORMAT command erases the contents of a diskette, so be sure to use a blank diskette or one that is no longer needed.

When the SYSGEN command is executed, a copy of the operating system is recorded on the diskette. This allows the working copy to be used to "start up" the computer. The master diskette is "write protected" and does not contain a copy of CP/M. As a result, the master Perfect Filer diskette generally cannot be used.

When the Kaypro computer is powered on, the following message will be displayed:

```
*KAYPRO II*

Please insert your diskette into Drive A
```

When the Perfect Filer diskette has been inserted in drive A, the following message should appear:

```
KAYPRO II
64k CP/M v 2.2

A>
```

If this message does not appear, be sure that your working copy contains a copy of the operating system.

In response to the system prompt, enter the following command:

A>FILER

This command should generate the following prompt:

```
Perfect Filer  1.0
Copyright (c) 1982 by Perfect Software, Inc.
KAYPRO II Terminal
Enter disk drive containing data base:
```

The Perfect Filer program is now ready to be used.

**Data Bases**

A **data base** is a set of information that is available to a computer operator. The data bases that are used with the Perfect Filer program are merely a collection of entries in a file.

Two different data bases are provided with the Perfect Filer program. These are called the *individual member data base* and the *organizational data base.*

The individual member data base is specifically designed for data that is organized according to a particular set of people. The individual member data base is similar in concept to a personal address book.

The organizational data base is organized according to groups or companies. A file that includes information about all the firms in a particular industry is an example of an organizational data base.

If the two data bases that are provided with the Perfect Filer program are not appropriate for a particular application, additional data bases can be created. The Perfect Filer program can be used to create data bases for a vast number of data storage requirements.

## Concept

The Perfect Filer program allows a large amount of information to be stored in an orderly manner. The program allows the data to be recovered in a variety of ways. Furthermore, the information can be sorted in several different ways to allow fast and orderly recovery of the information.

The program also allows the information stored in the data base to be used in form letters. For example the name and address of many clients can be included in a standard letter automatically.

## Procedure

The Perfect Filer diskette includes the individual member data base. As a result, the Perfect Filer diskette is the only diskette needed to use that data base.

The organizational data base resides on the Installation Disk for the Perfect Writer. In order to use the organizational data base, the Filer Disk must be inserted in drive A, and the Installation Disk must be inserted in drive B.

When the Perfect Filer program is executed, the original prompt asks for the user to specify the disk drive that contains the database. Generally, the individual member data base will be used on drive A, and the organizational data base will be used on drive B.

**Prompts**

The Perfect Filer program uses the character X to choose selections from a menu. When a set of options is displayed, a blinking X character appears at the left of the first option.

When the X key is pressed, the option that has the blinking X on the same line is chosen. The X on the display is moved down one line on the menu whenever the Return key is pressed. The X moves up one line each time the Backspace key is pressed.

For example, a typical Perfect Filer menu appears as follows:

```
X Access Individuals Members
  Generate List/Report
  Generate Mail
  Define Subset
  Define List Format
  Define Printer Form
```

In order to choose the Generate Mail selection from this menu, press the Return key twice to move the blinking X prompt down to the third line.

The menu now appears as follows:

```
  Access Individual Members
  Generate List/Report
X Generate Mail
  Define Subset
  Define List Format
  Define Printer Form
```

When the blinking X prompt appears to the left of the desired selection, press the X key in order to choose the selection.

**The Escape Key**

The Escape Key (ESC) is used in the Perfect Filer program to "back up" to the previous level. When the program is executed, it proceeds through several levels of operations. When the ESC key is used, the program retracts to the precedng level.

If the ESC key is pressed several times in a row, the computer backs out of the Perfect Filer and into CP/M. When the message "Warm Boot" and the system prompt (A>) are displayed, the FILER command must be executed before Perfect Filer can be used again.

**Changing the Date**

When the disk drive that contains the database is specified, the Perfect Writer program begins automatically.

The first screen that is displayed is used to enter the correct date. The current date is displayed at the top of the screen, along with the selections Date Correct and Change Date.

If the current date is correct, simply press the X key to proceed with the program. If the current date is not correct, press the Return key to move the prompt to the other selection, then press the X key to choose the Change Date option.

When the Change Date selection is executed, the user is prompted to enter the number of the current month, day and year. The following is a typical date entry sequence.

```
Enter Today's Date:
Enter month: 6
Enter day: 21
Enter year: 83
```

When the date entry is complete, the user is asked if the new date is correct. If a mistake has been made, the same process can be repeated.

## ACCESSING INDIVIDUAL MEMBERS

The second menu that will be displayed contains six selections. The first selection is Access Individual Members. This selection allows a member to be added, deleted or updated.

The two data bases have different configurations of information for the entries. This is the only difference between the data bases.

Illustration 5-1 contains the format of an individual member data base entry, and Illustration 5-2 contains the format of an organizational data base entry.

**Illustration 5-1. Individual Data Base Format**

First Name: Middle: Last:
Title: Salutation: (Dear) Title 2:

Organization:
Address 1:
Address 2:
City: State: Zip:
Country:

Home Phone: ( ) - Active [ ]
Business Phone: ( ) -

Comment 1:
Comment 2:

Date Entered: / /

**Illustration 5-2. Organizational Data Base Format**

Organization:
Address 1:
Address 2:
City: State: Zip:
Country:

Phone: ( ) -

Contact Person: Active [ ]

Comment:
:

Date Entered: / /

When the Access Individual Members is selected, the following 3 selections are displayed on the monitor.

Add a New Member

Review/Update Existing Member

Delete Member

**Adding a New Member**

When the Add a New Member selection is chosen, a blank data base entry appears on the screen as depicted in Illustrations 5-1 and 5-2.

Data is entered into a data base entry directly from the keyboard. Simply type in the desired information and use the Return key to proceed to the next data item. If it is necessary to return to a previous data item within the entry, use the ↑ key to move backward.

Each section of the entry where data can be entered is called a field. The ← and → keys can be used to move the cursor left and right within a field. The ↑ and ↓ keys can be used to move the cursor to a preceding or subsequent field.

When an entry appears exactly as it should be saved in the data base, hold down the CRTL key and type E.

The Perfect Filer automatically proceeds with another blank entry on the display. When you no longer wish to make entries to the data base, press the ESC key.

If the ESC key is pressed while an entry is being made (but not saved), the Perfect Filer will not proceed until the user responds to the following prompt.

Confirm Discard of Recent Input

DISCARD Input to Member

Save Input to Member

If the first selection is chosen, the last entry is not saved. If the second selection is made, the entry is saved before the program continues.

## UDATING AND REVIEWING ENTRIES

The second way to access individual members of the data base is to use the Update/Review selection. When updating an entry, the members are called individually from the data base. The two different data bases use two different methods to distinguish the elements.

The individual member data base uses the person's first initial along with the first three letters of their last name. For example, any of the following individuals could be designated by JGRA.

Joan Gray
James Gravely
Joseph Grazak

The organizational data base uses the first four letters of the organization's name to distinguish the entries on file. For example, JONE could be used to designate any of the following entries.

Jones Towing
Jonesco Products, Inc.
Jonelis Moving and Storage

When the Update/Review selection has been chosen, the prompt will ask for the four characters that are used to specify an entry in the data base.

When the specifier has been entered, the entry of an organization or individual will be displayed on the monitor. If the specifier does not match any of the entries in the data base, the following message appears on the display.

```
No such member
Hit any character to continue.
```

If the specifier matches more than one entry, the command Control-O can be used to view another entry that has the same specifier. If the Control-O command is used when no other members have the same specifier, the following message will be displayed.

```
No more members
Hit any character to continue.
```

### Deleting an Entry

An entry can be deleted by choosing the Delete Member option. In the Delete mode, the same four letter specifier will be used to select an entry.

When the specifier is entered, the following message will be displayed on the screen.

```
You will be shown a data display screen--
to delete the member displayed Type Control D
Hit any character to continue
```

The Perfect Filer proceeds by displaying an entry that has the denoted specifier. In order to delete an entry, press the D key while holding down the CTRL key. To proceed with another entry, execute the Control-O command. Once again, the message "No more members" will be displayed if all of the entries with the denoted specifier have already been displayed.

It is not necessary to delete any files while in the delete mode. Either Control-O or Escape can be used to proceed with the program without actually deleting any entries.

## GENERATING LISTS

The Generate List/Report option can be used to output a portion of the data in the data base. This option is capable of producing lists of the members in a data base as well as their addresses. The list can be sorted according to the name, city, state or zip code of the entries.

## List Formats

The organizational and individual member data bases use the same procedure to generate lists. The entries in the data base can be sorted in 5 different ways.

The first list format simply prints the names of the members of the data base in alphabetical order.

The second format prints the names and addresses of the members according to the alphabetical order of the names.

The third format outputs the names and addresses of the members in alphabetical order according to the cities of the members. The members are arranged in alphabetical order by name beneath the heading of each city.

The fourth format arranges the list in alphabetical order according to the state, city and name of the members in the data base.

The last format arranges the output according to the zip codes and names of the entries.

## Subsets

Both the organized and individual member data bases have a field labeled Active [ ] (see Illustrations 5-1 and 5-2). If the letter X is entered between the square brackets, the member is considered active. If no character is entered between the brackets, the member is considered inactive.

When the List/Report option has been specified, the active/inactive status is taken into account. After the format selection has been chosen, the following selections will be available.

```
Select Subset to List
            All Members
            Inactive Members
            Active Members
```

If the Inactive Members selection was chosen, only the entries that do not have an X in the Active field will be included in the list. Conversely, if the Active Members selection was chosen, only the members that have an X in the Active field will be included in the list.

**List Targets**

The next menu that appears on the display is used to select the type of output of the list. The list can be either sent to the display, printer or a disk file. The List Targets menu appears as follows.

```
Select List Targets
            CRT→ON
            Printer→ OFF
            File→OFF
            Sort Image→OFF
```

The File selection can be used to output an actual copy of the list in a specified file. The Sort Image selection can be used to output the results of the list in a special output file. The Sort Image file cannot be output because the file is written in a special code that only Perfect Filer understands. A Sort Image file is used when a form letter is to be sent to the members on the list.

When the blinking X prompt is used to activate one of the output devices, the OFF message changes to ON. Any or all of the output devices can be used simultaneously. When the File or Sort Image options are selected, a file name for the output must be specified.

When the List Targets menu appears on the display the Escape (ESC) key is used to begin the output procedure. Generally, Escape is used to "back up", but in this case, Escape is used to "go ahead."

## GENERATING MAIL

The Perfect Filer program can be used to generate mail for the members of the data base. Any of the information that is entered for the members can be recalled in the context of a letter or memo.

Each data item in a data base entry is assigned a name. When the particular data name is included in a letter, the actual information will be taken from the data base and inserted into the letter. Tables 5-1 and 5-2 contain the names that are used to designate the individual data items in the two standard data bases.

The first part of an information name describes the general category of the data. The second part denotes the specific type of information.

If the first part of an information name is used, all of the information in the entire category will be included in the file.

For example, use the Perfect Writer program to create a file with the contents of Illustration 5-3. This file will be used to generate a letter that includes the information in the individual member data base.

**Table 5-1. Individual Member Data Base Information Names**

| Field Name | Information Name | Field Name | Information Name |
|---|---|---|---|
| First Name | name.firstname | Country | address.country |
| Middle | name.middlename | Home Phone (area code) | homephone.areacd |
| Last | name.lastname | Home Phone (number) | homephone.phnum |
| Title 1 | name.title | Active | active |
| Salutation | name.salutation | Business Phone (area code) | busphone.areacd |
| Title 2 | name.title 2 | Business Phone (number) | busphone.phnum |
| Organization | address.organization | Comment 1 | comment1 |
| Address 1 | address.address 1 | Comment 2 | comment2 |
| Address 2 | address.address 2 | Date Entered (month) | dtenter.month |
| City | address.city | Date Entered (day) | dtenter.day |
| State | address.state | Date Entered (year) | dtenter.year |
| Zip | address.zip | | |

**Table 5-2. Organizational Data Base Information Names**

| Field Name | Information Name | Field Name | Info. Name |
|---|---|---|---|
| Organization | address.organization | Phone (number) | phone.phnum |
| Address 1 | address.address 1 | Contact | contact |
| Address 2 | address.address 2 | Active | active |
| City | address.city | Comment 1 | comment 1 |
| State | address.state | Comment 2 | comment 2 |
| Zip | address.zip | Date Entered (month) | dtenter.month |
| Country | address.country | Date Entered (day) | dtenter.day |
| Phone (area code) | phone.areacd | Date Entered (year) | dtenter.year |

Since the Perfect Writer diskette must eventually be replaced with the Perfect Filer diskette, create the file on a diskette in drive B. Be sure to use the drive specifier B: in the file name.

Do not use the TAB key when creating mail files. The TAB key causes problems when the Generate Mail function is executed. When a file that uses the TAB function is executed, the following error message is displayed.

Bad character [Ascii 9]

**Special Information Names**

No matter what data base is used with the Perfect Filer program, the current data can be included in a file by using the information name "today." When this information name is used, the month is written, followed by the day and year. For example, the date would appear in an output file as follows if the "today" information name is used.

November 12, 1981

Another special information name is "salutation (name)." This is used only with the individual data base to include the word Dear, followed by the data item that appears in the salutation field. For example, if the salutation field contains the name Steve, the "salutation (name)" information name will generate the following results:

Dear Steve

**Using Information Names**

Information names are used in document files to include information that is stored in a data base. Illustration 5-3 depicts a form letter that uses several information names.

**Illustration 5-3. A Sample File for Generating Mail**

<today>

<name>
<address>

<salutation(name)>,

I am looking forward to meeting with you during my upcoming visit to <address.city>.

If you need to make any revisions in our plans, please contact my secretary.

Sincerely,

William Jones

Make note of the use of angle brackets in the file. Any information name that appears in the file must be enclosed in these brackets.

The first item in the file is an information name that is used to insert the current date in the final output letter.

The second and third items are used to specify the name and complete address of the member in the data base.

Since the information name only includes the general type of information, the entire name and address are included in the output.

The salutation information name is used to insert the word "Dear" as well as the name specified in the salutation field of the data base entry.

The fifth information name is "address.city." This name is used to insert the city of the member of the data base in the output.

This file can be used with the Perfect Filer to generate a letter with the following format.

June 23, 1983

Stephen Szczecinski
Weber Systems Inc.
8437 Mayfield Road
Chesterland, OH 44026

Dear Steve,

I am looking forward to meeting with you during my upcoming visit to Chesterland.

If you need to make any revisions in our plans, please contact my secretary.

Sincerely,

William Jones

**Generating Output**

When the Generate Mail selection is chosen from the original menu, another set of selections are displayed on the screen. The selection of choices appears as follows.

One Inch One-Across Labels
Single Sheet Letters
Single Envelopes
Continuous Letterhead
Continuous Envelopes

These selections are used to specify the type of printer form that is to be used for the output.

The first selection is chosen when the Perfect Filer is to be used to output mailing labels.

The second selection is chosen when each piece of paper is to be inserted into the printer individually.

The third selection is to be used when individual envelopes are being addressed.

The fourth selection is to be used when the printer paper is continuous.

The fifth selection is to be chosen when continuous envelopes are addressed.

When a selection is made from the printer form menu, the following prompt appears at the top of the display.

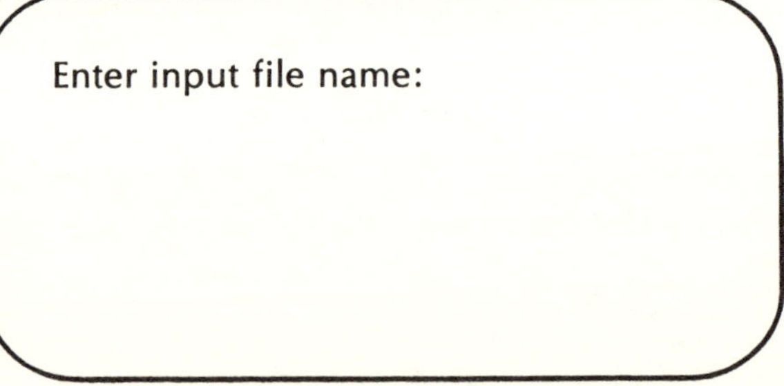


In response to this prompt, enter the name of the file that is to be used for generating mail. Be sure to use the drive specifier B: if the file diskette is in drive B. The file is used to generate mail exactly as it appears in the file.

When the filename is specified, a menu will be displayed with the choices of output devices. The Mail Target menu is used in the same way as the List Target menu. The menu appears as follows.

CRT→ON
Printer→OFF
File → OFF

When the blinking X prompt is used to actuate one of the output devices, the OFF message changes to ON. Since all of the output devices can be used simultaneously, this menu is not cleared when a selection is made. This allows the menu to be used more than once when the output devices are being selected.

In order to exit the Mail Target menu, press the ESC key. When this menu has been exited, the mail will be output to the appropriate output devices.

The output automatically appears on the display, so the CRT selection on the menu has no effect.

If the printer was selected, be sure that the printer is powered on and ready to operate. If the printer selection was chosen without the printer being connected, the Perfect Filer will not be able to continue.

If the file selection was chosen, the name of the output file must also be specified. When a disk file is used as the output device, the following prompt will appear on the display.

Enter output file name:

Be sure to use the drive specifier B: when appropriate.

When a file has been selected as the output device, the output can be placed in a new file, or added to an existing file. Either of these selections can be made when the following two selections appear on the display.

Create New File

Append to Existing File

If you wish to add the output to an existing file, be sure that the specified output file already exists.

The Perfect Filer program has the capability of generating mail according to the information in any entry of the data base. There are three methods that can be used to specify the members of a data base that are to receive an item of mail. The three methods of specifying recipients of mail are displayed on a menu as follows.

Individually by Member ID

By Subset

From Sort Image

The first method used to specify mail recipients is the Individual ID method. When this selection method is chosen, the Perfect Filer uses the four character identification code to access data base members. After the four letter code has been entered, an entry from the data base that corresponds to the code will be displayed on the monitor. If you would like to send the mail to the member whose entry appears on the display, type Y. If you do not want to send mail, type N. When N is entered, another entry from the data base will be displayed as long as another member matches the specified identification code.

The second method of specifying mail recipients is by subset. The standard data bases use the Active field on each entry to divide the data base into 3 subsets. When the "By Subset" selection is chosen, another menu will appear on the display. This menu allows the mail to be sent to all members, inactive members, or active members only.

The third method of specifying mail recipients is with a Sort Image. Recall from the section on generating lists that a sort image consists of a portion of the data base that has been organized according to city, state, zip code, etc. Once a sort image has been created with the Generate List command, it will be stored in a disk file until it can be used to generate mail. Once the "From Sort Image" selection has been chosen, the name of the diskette file that contains the sort image must be specified. Be sure to use the drive specifier B: when appropriate. When this last step has been completed, the mail will be generated at the appropriate output devices.

## CREATING A NEW DATA BASE

If one of the two data bases provided with the Perfect Filer are not sufficient for your needs, a new data base can be created quickly and easily.

There are a few limitations that must be considered when creating a data base. Each data base entry is limited to the size of the display screen. In other words, the data base entry can not exceed 24 lines in total or 80 characters in any one line. Also, each entry must not contain more than 70 data fields. The number of spaces used to contain data in each entry must not exceed 1024. This same limit (1024 spaces) applies to the total of the data descriptions as well. The most important limitation is the fact that each data base must be contained on its own diskette.

To create a data base, insert the Perfect Filer diskette in drive A and a blank, formatted diskette in drive B. Press the Reset switch in order to initialize the system. When the system prompt (A>) appears on the display, execute the CREATE command.

A>CREATE

When this command has been executed, the following prompt will appear on the display.

```
Create  v1.0
Perfect Filer  v1.0
Copyright (c) 1982 by Perfect Software, Inc.
Kaypro II          Terminal
CP/M version 2.X
Enter data base disk drive:
```

In response to the prompt, enter B followed by Return.

The Data Base Generation menu will appear on the display. Choose the "Create New Data Base" selection. Another prompt will appear on the display as follows.

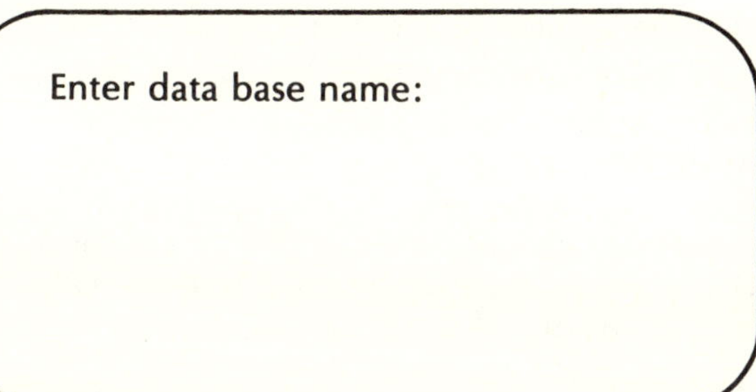


Enter a convenient title for the data base. The name of our example data base is "Inventory".

Once the data base has been named, choose the "Define Data Display Screen" selection from the menu. At this point, the screen will be cleared in order to display the format of the new data base entries.

Before a data base can actually be created, it is necessary to understand some of the features of Perfect Filer. The most important aspects of the program are discussed in the following sections.

**Templates**

A template is a predefined set of data fields for a data base entry. Templates are provided with the Perfect Filer program to aid in the creating of new data bases.

The categories of available templates are as follows:

NAME
ADDRESS
PHONE NUMBER
SOCIAL SECURITY NUMBER
DATE
DATE ENTERED
TIME
MONEY

The data base is not limited to the predefined templates. Any type of data field can be created to accept any type of data.

## Types of Fields

There are four types of data that can be assigned to a field. Since the type of data must be specified when a data base is defined, the Perfect Filer will not allow an incorrect type of data to be assigned to field.

The four types of data are as follows:

alphanumeric
alphabetic
numeric
status

The most general type of data is alphanumeric. This type of data includes all of the numbers and letters, as well as all the special characters.

Alphabetic data is restricted to the letters A through Z. When a field is defined as alphabetic, any numbers, punctuation, or special characters cannot be assigned to the field.

Numeric data is restricted to the numbers 0 through 9. Numeric fields cannot contain letters, punctuation, or special characters.

Status data can consist only of the letter X. This type of data is generally used to indicate if a data base member belongs in a particular category. An example of status data are the "Active" fields in the Organizational and Individual Member data bases. Status fields are convenient to use for generating lists of particular members of a data base. For example, the "Active" status field can be used to generate lists of active members.

**Field Sizes**

When a field is selected, the size of the field must also be specified. A field should be large enough to accept the proper amount of data, but small enough to allow enough room for the other data fields in the data base entries.

**Restricted Values**

When a numeric field is created, the Perfect Filer program asks for the maximum and minimum values that can be entered in the field. This feature helps prevent incorrect data from being entered. The computer beeps and does not allow a data item outside this range to be entered.

**Creating a Data Base Entry**

When the display has been cleared and the cursor appears at the upper left corner of the screen, Perfect Filer is ready to begin accepting data field descriptions.

The following data base entry will be described in our example:

Part number:
Description:
Cost: $ .
Quantity:

Begin by typing the first data description "Part Number: ".* Be sure to include an extra space at the end of each description in order to make the entry easier to read.

After the description has been entered, execute the following command:

Control-I

---

* It isn't necessary to include the quotation marks in the data descriptions.

This command allows the user to specify the data description. The program will proceed to the "Select field type" menu. Since the Part Number field only includes the digits 0 through 9, choose the "Numeric Field" selection.

The next prompt asks the user to enter the field tag. The field tag is a convenient name that can be used to reference the data within a form letter or a list. A convenient tag for this field would be "partnumber".

The next prompt asks for the number of spaces that the specified data field requires. Four spaces would be a convenient value to enter for the size of the Part Number field.

Two more prompts appear to specify the minimum and maximum values that can be accepted in the field. Specify a minimum value of 0 and a maximum value of 9999. These values allow ten thousand different part numbers to be assigned.

When the "Part Number" field has been entered, press the Return key twice in order to skip a line before the next entry is made. Proceed by typing the word "Description: ". Once again, press Control-I to insert the data description into the data base entry.

The "Select field type" menu will again be displayed on the screen. The "Alphanumeric Field" selection should be chosen because the description of the part may contain letters or numbers.

When the "Enter field tag" prompt appears on the display, enter "description", followed by the Return key. When the "Enter field length" prompt appears, enter 50, or some other convenient value.

When the first two data descriptions have been entered, the display should appear as follows:

Part Number: ....

Description: ..................................................

Proceed by pressing the Return key twice in order to move to a new line of output. Type the data description "Cost: $". Enter the Control-I command to insert the data descriptors into the data base.

When the "select field type" menu appears on the display, choose the "Numeric Field" selection. As the prompts appear on the display, enter the field tag "dollar", and enter a field length of "3". Specify a minimum value of 0, and a maximum value of 999. These selections cause negative numbers or numbers greater than 999 to be rejected.

The last line of the entry should now appear as follows:

Cost: $...

Since the cursor is located one space to the right of the dollar sign, use the cursor-right key (→) to move three spaces forward. The cursor should now be located at the decimal point location.

Simply press the period key ( . ) and proceed by executing the insert command: Control-I. Choose the "Numeric Field" selection from the "Select field type" menu. Enter the field tag "cent" when the field tag prompt appears on the display. Choose a field length of "2", a minimum value of 0 and a maximum value of 99. The last line of the entry should now appear as follows:

Cost: $.......

The final data description in the data base entry is the quantity. Press the Return key twice and type the description "Quantity: ". Press Control-I and choose the "Numeric Field" selection from the "Select field type" menu. Proceed by entering a field tag of "qty" and a field length of "4". Specify a minimum value of 0 and a maximum value of 9999.

When the Quantity entry has been finished, the data base entry is complete. The display should now appear as follows:

```
Part Number: ....
Description:.............................................
Cost: $ ....--
Quantity: ....
```

Press the ESC key in order to exit the CREATE mode of Perfect Filer. When the following menu appears on the display, choose the "Save Data Base" selection:

```
Inventory
          Define Data Display Screen
          Display Screen Definition
          Set System Parameters
          Save Data Base
```

When this selection has been chosen, the following message appears on the display.

```
WARNING: The database on disk b is about to be initialized.
Any existing data there will be lost.
To Abort now, hit ESCape; to continue hit any other character
```

Since the data base is newly created, it does not contain any information yet. As a result, this warning should not concern anyone who created a new data base. Simply press any key to continue.

While the data base is being written, a great deal of technical information will be displayed on the monitor. This information is simply a review of the definitions of the database.

When the data base has been completely saved, the disk drives will stop operating and the following prompt will appear at the bottom of the display:

```
Press any key to continue.
```

When the program continues, the "Data Base Generation" menu will appear on the display. Press the ESC key to exit the CREATE program. Once again, the system prompt (A>) is displayed on the display.

To begin using the new data base, execute the FILER program.

A>FILER

When the Perfect Filer prompt appears on the display, enter the disk drive that contains the data base. The data base is used in the same manner as the organizational data base or the individual member data base.

The data will be entered in the same way, but when the members are reviewed or updated, each member must be specified by the part number.

Since the part number is the first data field in the entry, the first four numbers will be used to specify a member. Since the data field has only four numbers, the entire part number will be used to specify the members.

The "Generate List/Report" command can not be utilized with a new data base until a list format has been defined.

## OTHER FEATURES

Defining a list format can become a tedious procedure. However, this feature can be used to generate packing slips, invoices, inventory reports, and much more. Also a great deal of sort options can also be used with the Perfect Filer program.

This chapter does not include all of the features of the Perfect Filer. For an explanation of the more sophisticated capabilities of the program, consult the **Perfect Filer User's Guide.**

# CHAPTER 6.
# PERFECT CALC

---

## INTRODUCTION

The Perfect Calc program is a versatile tool that can be used to simplify any type of calculation. This program utilizes a worksheet that allows calculations to be performed quickly, accurately, and in an orderly fashion. Any project that includes tedious calculations can be simplified by the Perfect Calc program.

### Getting Started

The Perfect Calc master diskette is included in the standard software package provided with the Kaypro computer. In order to make a working copy of the master diskette, perform the FORMAT, COPY and SYSGEN procedures as described in Chapter 2. Since the FORMAT command erases the contents of a diskette, always be sure that any information on the diskette is no longer needed.

The master diskette should be promptly stored in a safe place after a working copy has been made.

When the computer is powered on, the following message will be displayed.

```
*KAYPRO II*

Please insert your diskette into Drive A
```

When the Perfect Calc diskette has been booted in drive A, the following message should appear.

```
KAYPRO II
64K CP/M v 2.2

A>
```

If this message does not appear, be sure that your working copy diskette contains a copy of the operating system.

When the system prompt (A>) appears, the Perfect Calc program can be accessed from CP/M. Each Perfect Calc worksheet is stored in its own disk file with a filename containing 8 or fewer characters and an optional filename extension. It is recommended that the filename extension PC be included with all Perfect Calc filenames. Remember that the filename will be needed to reload the worksheet in the future.

In order to begin a Perfect Calc worksheet, a filename must be assigned by using the following statement:

A>PC *filename*.PC

The program can be accessed simply by entering PC in response to the system prompt, but this is generally a bad idea. When this command is used, the file will automatically be assigned the filename DEFAULT.PC. This file is saved on the diskette in disk drive A only until another DEFAULT file is created. Since it is generally a good idea to create files on the diskette in drive B, the PC command should not be used.

After a PC command has been executed with an appropriate filename, the original worksheet will appear as depicted in Illustration 6-1.

**Illustration 6-1. The Original Worksheet**

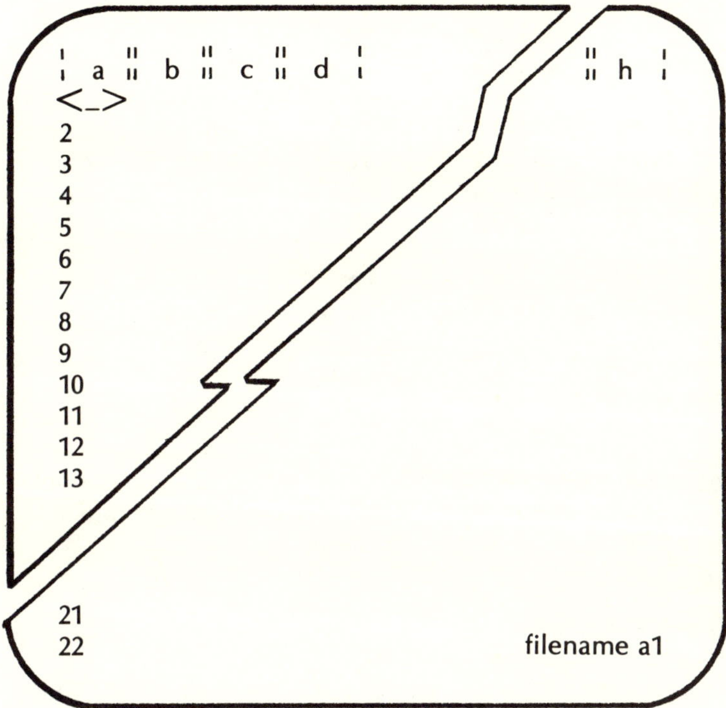


A typical application of the Perfect Calc program is depicted in Illustration 6-2.

**Illustration 6-2. A Typical Application of Perfect Calc.**

| Date | Initial Mileage | Final Mileage | Gallons | MPG |
|---|---|---|---|---|
| ------------- | ------------- | ------------- | ------------- | ------------- |
| 6-04-83 | 53347.4 | 53521.5 | 9.8 | 17.8 |
| 6-11-83 | 53521.5 | 53701.4 | 10.2 | 17.6 |
| 6-18-83 | 53701.4 | 53992.5 | 16.2 | 18.0 |
| 6-25-83 | 53992.5 | 54189.3 | 11.0 | 17.9 |

| TOTALS | |
|---|---|
| Miles | 841.9 |
| Gallons | 47.2 |
| MPG | 17.8 |

This table will be used throughout this chapter as an example of the various techniques used to perform calculations with Perfect Calc.

## Moving the Cursor

The cursor consists of a pair of angle brackets (〈 〉). These are used to indicate the location where the next item of information will be entered on the table. The cursor control commands are very similar to the commands used with the Perfect Writer program.

Each position on the table is designated by a letter and number to specify the column and row of each entry. Although 8 columns and 22 rows are displayed on the original worksheet, the entire worksheet contains 52 columns and 255 rows. Due to the size of the worksheet, only a small portion can appear on the display at any time. The commands that are used to move the cursor and view different parts of the worksheet are displayed in Table 6-1.

**Table 6-1. Cursor Control Commands***

| Key | Action |
|---|---|
| → | Move one column to the right |
| ← | Move one column to the left |
| ↑ | Move up one line |
| ↓ | Move down one line |
| Control-A | Move to the beginning of the line |
| Control-E | Move to the end of the line |
| Escape,< | Move to the top of the column |
| Escape,> | Move to the bottom of the column |
| Control-V | Move down one page |
| Control-Z | Move up one page |
| Escape, V | Move one page to the right |
| Escape,Z | Move one page to the left |

The GOTO command can be used to move the cursor to a specific location. The GOTO command is represented by the "greater than" symbol (>). When this command is executed, the following prompt will appear at the bottom of the display.

GO TO:

In response to this prompt, enter a column letter and row number. For example, a1, f5 and z255 are all acceptable responses to the prompt.

### Data

The data entered in the table can be one of three types. The data can be a number, label or formula. Numbers are the numberic values that are entered in the table. Labels are the

---

* The notations used to describe the commands follow the same conventions described in earlier chapters. The "Control" commands consist of holding down the key labeled CTRL while pressing another key. The "Escape" commands consist of pressing and releasing the key labeled ESC, then pressing another key.

words, symbols or special characters that are used to make the table easy to read. Formulae are used to calculate results from the other values on the table.

Whenever an entry is made, one of the following prompts will appear at the bottom of the display in order to indicate the type of information being entered.

LABEL:
NUMBER:
FORMULA:

When an entry begins with a digit, decimal point, or minus sign, the data is automatically considered a number. Numbers are used in the table with 13 digits of accuracy. Although 13 digits will not necessarily appear on the display, the computer will use all of the digits when calculations are performed.

Any entry that begins with a character other than the digits 0-9, minus sign, decimal point or equal sign is automatically considered a label. A label is entered on the display exactly as it is typed. The double quotation mark (") is used to signal the computer that the next value should be considered a label. This allows a character string beginning with the digits 0-9, minus sign, decimal point or equal sign to be a label. The double quote does not appear in the label.

A formula is defined for the current cursor position by entering an equal sign. When an equal sign is entered, the word FORMULA: is displayed at the bottom of the display, followed by the current cursor location and an equal sign. The following example is a typical prompt that will appear when an equal sign is entered.

FORMULA:a1=

A formula uses values of other locations in the worksheet to calculate the value for its specified location. A formula can contain the standard algebraic, relational or logical operations. There are many additional functions that are available for calculating values.

The operations and functions that are used with the Perfect Calc program are summarized in Table 6-2 and 6-3.

**Table 6-2. Perfect Calc Operators**

| | |
|---|---|
| ↑ Exponentiation | < Less than |
| * Multiplication | <= Less than or equal |
| / Division | = Equal |
| + Addition | <> Not Equal |
| - Subtraction | > Greater than |
| | >= Greater than or equal |

**Table 6-3. Perfect Calc Functions**

| | |
|---|---|
| abs (argument) | Returns the absolute value of the argument. |
| and (argument 1, argument 2) | Returns the value 1 if both arguments are non-zero. Otherwise the value 0 is returned. |
| atan (argument) | Returns the arctangent of the argument (in radians). |
| avg (range) | Returns the mean value of the specified range. |
| cos (argument) | Returns the cosine of the argument (in radians). |
| count (range) | Returns the number of valid entries in the specified range. |
| exp (argument) | Returns the value of e (2.7182...) raised to the power of the argument. |
| if (argument, value 1, value 2) | Returns value 1 if X is non-zero. Otherwise, value 2 is returned. |
| int (argument) | Returns the smallest integer that is greater than the argument. |
| ln (argument) | Returns the natural logarithm of the argument. |
| log (argument) | Returns the base-10 logarithm of the argument. |
| lookup (value, range) | Searches a row or column specified by range and returns the value in the row column next to the specified value. |
| max (range) | Returns the largest value in the specified range. |

| | |
|---|---|
| min (range) | Returns the smallest value in a specified range. |
| not (argument) | Returns the value 0 if argument is non-zero, otherwise returns the value 1. |
| npv (rate, range) | Returns the net present value of values in the specified range, discounted at the specified rate. |
| or (argument 1, argument 2) | Returns the value 0 if both arguments are zero. Otherwise the value 1 is returned. |
| sqrt (argument) | Returns the square root of the argument. |
| sum (range) | Returns the sum of the values in the specified range. |

The arguments of a formula can be values, worksheet locations or regions of the worksheet. Locations that are used in formulae are simply designated by the column letter and line number.

A region of the worksheet can be specified by the first and last item in a row or column. Also, a set of values can be specified by the upper left and lower right corner values of the region. For example, the range a1:b3 would include the locations a1, a2, a3, b1, b2 and b3. This concept is demonstrated in Illustration 6-3.

The following formulae have the correct format for the Perfect Calc worksheet.

```
a11=npv(1,a1:a8)
b4=b1/(b2*100)
a9=sum(a1:a8)
b21=if(a15, b12, b13)
```

**Illustration 6-3. Defining Regions of the Worksheet**

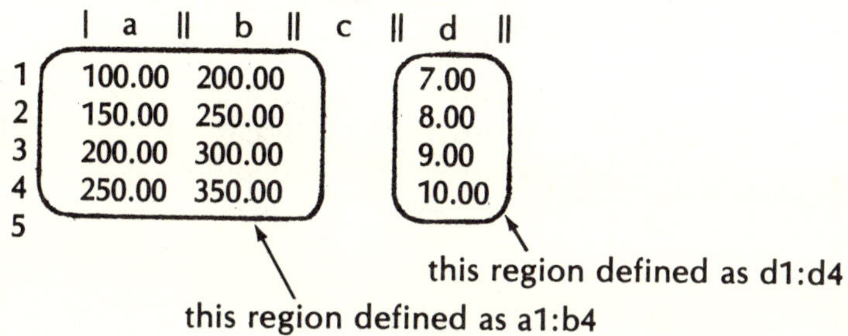


## SETTING UP THE SPREADSHEET

To begin setting up the worksheet, insert a working copy of the Perfect Calc master diskette in drive A and a blank, formatted diskette in drive B. Press the Reset switch to initialize the computer and generate the system prompt (A>). In response to the system prompt, enter the following command:

A>pc b:junempg.pc

When the program begins, the original worksheet will be displayed with the cursor positioned at location a1. At the bottom of the display, the message "New File" will be displayed. Also, the message "junempg a1" will be displayed to remind the user that the program name is "junempg" and that the cursor is positioned at location a1.

There are several commands that can be used to set the appearance of the worksheet. These commands can be used to change the column width, justify entries, set decimal places, etc. These commands are summarized in Table 6-4.

**Table 6-4. Spreadsheet Format Commands**

| | |
|---|---|
| Control-x,d | This command can be used to change the following display parameters.<br><br>The number of decimal places displayed (0 through 13)<br>Display numbers in scientific notation (press "s")<br>Display the worksheet formulae (press "f")<br>Display asterisks in bargraph style (press "*")<br>Display values in monetary notation with dollar sign and commas (press "$") |
| Control-x,j | This command is used to justify the entries in one of the following formats.<br><br>Left justification (press "l")<br>Right justification (press "r")<br>Center (press "c") |
| Control-x,t | This command is used to prevent the first column or first row from being scrolled off the display. This feature is convenient to use when the first row or column of the worksheet contain titles. This command requires one of the following three arguments.<br><br>Lock the first row in place (press "a")<br>Lock the first column in place (press "d")<br>Lock the first row and the first column (press "b") |
| Control-x,w | This command is used to select the width of a column. Any value from 0 through 76 can be specified. |

The Perfect Calc program will not accept upper case letters in format commands. Always be certain to use lower case letters in the Format mode. Finally, Format commands generally display a prompt that asks the user if the command should affect the entire worksheet (global) or affect only one line or column. The following prompt requires a response of "g", "l" or "c".

Global, Line, or Column?

The "g" selection cause the entire worksheet to be affected by the command. If the "l" or "c" selections are chosen, only the row or column where the cursor is currently located will be affected by the command.

To prepare the worksheet for the example in Illustration 6-2, two of the format commands must be executed.

The first command is used to specify the number of decimal places that are to appear on the worksheet. This command should have global effect since all of the numeric values contain only one value to the right of the decimal point.

Begin by executing the Control-x,d command, and press "g" when the following prompt appears.

Display: Global, Line, or Column?

When the "Global:" prompt appears, press the "1" key, and

press Return. This causes one decimal place to appear with all the numeric values throughout the worksheet.

The second command is used to cause the subsequent entries of the worksheet to appear in the center of each field. Begin by executing the Control-x,j command. When this command has been executed, the following prompt will appear at the bottom of the display.

```
Justify: Global, Line, or Column?
```

Since it's desirable to center the entries throughout the entire worksheet, press "g" in response to the preceding prompt. When the "Global:" prompt appears, press "c" to indicate that the entries should be centered.

The Justify and Display commands described above are both summarized in Table 6-4.

### Copying Entries

A powerful feature of the Perfect Calc program is its ability to copy entries that appear on the worksheet. This is accomplished with the Control-w and Control-y commands. In order to copy an entry, move the cursor to the position of the entry that is to be copied. Execute the Control-w command and proceed by moving the cursor to the location where the entry is to be placed. When the Control-y command is executed, a copy of the original entry will appear at the new cursor location.

### Entering Labels

Begin by using the ↓ key to move the cursor to position a3. Type the double quote (") character to indicate that the entry will be a label. When this character has been typed, the message "LABEL:" will appear at the bottom of the display. Type nine dashes to separate the column headings from the data. The last line on the display should appear as follows:

```
LABEL:---------
```

Press the Return key to place the entry on the worksheet.

Since the row of dashes is used beneath every column heading, the copy commands can be used to replicate the set of dashes. With the cursor located at position a3, execute the Control-w command. This command specifies that the entry at location a3 is to be copied. Proceed by using the → key to move the cursor to position b3. Execute the Control-y command to make a copy of the preceding entry.

Continue moving the cursor to the right and using the Control-y command until the line of dashes extends through the first 5 columns of the worksheet.

Move the cursor back three columns and up two lines to position b1. Type the entry "Initial". Since this entry begins with the letter I, it is automatically considered a label and the double quotation marks are not necessary. Press return to place in the entry on the worksheet.

Move the cursor forward one column to position c1. At this position enter "Final" in the same manner as "Initial" was entered. These labels are automatically entered on the worksheet when the Return key is pressed, or when the cursor is moved to a different location.

The upper left portion of the worksheet should appear as follows.

```
| a  || b  || c  || d  || e  |
1       Initial <Final>
2
3-----------------------------------------
```

Across line number 2 on the worksheet, make the following entries:

Date    Mileage    Mileage    Gallons    MPG

Simply move the cursor to the correct location and type the appropriate label.

If a mistake was made while entering an item in the worksheet, there are three ways the error can be corrected. If the entry has been typed incorrectly but not yet entered, use the DEL key to erase any mistakes. Then, retype the entry. If the item had already been entered in the worksheet, the Control-d command can be used to delete the entry where the cursor is located. Otherwise, simply make the correct entry with the cursor in the same position. Generally, the new entry will take the place of the old entry.

Proceed with the example worksheet by entering the four dates in column a, rows 4 through 7. Since the dates begin with a number, the double quote (") must be the first character entered to indicate that these entries are labels. When the entries have been completed, the worksheet should appear as follows:

```
  |  a   ||   b    ||   c    ||   d    ||  e  |
1            Initial    Final
2   Date    Mileage   Mileage  Gallons    MPG
3-------------------------------------------------
4  6-04-83
5  6-11-83
6  6-18-83
<  6-25-83 >
```

Use the → and ↓ keys to move the cursor to location c9 and enter the label "TOTALS". Move the cursor down one row and enter the label "Miles". It is convenient to right justify the entries beneath the "TOTALS" heading. Execute the justify command (Control-x,j) and specify "l" for line and "r" for right justify.

Continue by moving the cursor down one row and entering the label "Gallons". Once again, use the Control-x,j,l,r command sequence to right justify the entries in this line.

Move down one more line to position c11 and enter the label "MPG". Continue by executing the same right justification command. Now that all the labels on the worksheet are entered, the newly entered labels should appear as follows:

```
TOTALS
         Miles
       Gallons
           MPG
```

**Entering Numbers**

Use the ← and ↑ keys to move the cursor to the first position under the Initial Mileage heading (position b4). At this location, enter the value 53347.4. When this value has been entered, the following message should appear at the bottom of the display.

```
NUMBER: 53347.4
```

When the Return key has been pressed, or the cursor moved to the next position, the value at the bottom of the worksheet will be entered at the current location of the cursor.

Move the cursor to the Final Mileage column and enter the following values.

53521.5
53701.4
53992.5
54189.3

Be sure to move the cursor down one row after each value is entered.

When all of the Final Mileage values are entered, use the ↑ and → keys to move the cursor to the top of the Gallons column (position d4). Enter the following four values in the locations d4 through d7.

9.8
10.2
16.2
11.0

When these values have been entered, the data entry portion of the worksheet will have been completed. The remaining values in the worksheet are to be calculated from the existing data. The top half of the worksheet should now appear as follows:

| | a | b | c | d | e |
|---|---|---|---|---|---|
| 1 | | Initial | Final | | |
| 2 | Date | Mileage | Mileage | Gallons | MPG |
| 3 | ---------- | ---------- | ---------- | ---------- | ---------- |
| 4 | 6-04-83 | 53347.4 | 53521.5 | 9.8 | |
| 5 | 6-11-83 | | 53701.4 | 10.2 | |
| 6 | 6-18-83 | | 53992.5 | 16.2 | |
| 7 | 6-25-83 | | 54189.3 | 11.0 | |

## Entering Formulae

Formulae are entered in the worksheet by typing an equal sign (=) followed by a series of one or several values, worksheet locations, functions or operators. Table 6-2 and 6-3 include a summary of the Perfect Calc functions and operations.

Formulae can be copied from one location and placed in another using the Control-w and Control-y commands. Begin this procedure by entering the original formula, pressing Return, and then executing the Control-w command. When the cursor is moved to the new location, simply execute the Control-y command. When this procedure is used, a prompt will appear at the bottom of the display questioning whether the positions specified in the formula are relative or absolute.

For example, if a column is calculated as the percent of total sales for each quarter of a year, a worksheet may appear as follows:

| | a | b | c |
|---|---|---|---|
| 1 | | Sales | Percent |
| 2 | 1st qtr | 1,000 | 21.1 |
| 3 | 2nd qtr | 1,200 | 25.3 |
| 4 | 3rd qtr | 1,450 | 30.5 |
| 5 | 4th qtr | 1,100 | 23.2 |
| 6 | | ------ | ---- |
| 7 | total | 4,750 | 100.0 |

In order to compute the value of location c2, the following formula could be used.

c2 = 100*b2/b7

To make a copy of this formula for location c3, it would be desirable to use the same formula except using b3 in place of b2. In this example, the location b7 is not a relative variable. However, if b2 is declared a relative variable, the same formula can be copied for rows 3, 4 and 5 in the worksheet.

If a formula contains several variables, the prompt at the bottom of the page requires a response to the Relative? question for each variable. The particular variable in question is designated by a reverse set of angle brackets (><).

There are several responses that can be used when the Relative? prompt is displayed. Y and N are used to represent yes and no. The DEL key is used to begin the prompt again, starting with the first variable. The exclamation mark (!) is used to indicate that the previous response should be repeated for all the remaining variables.

To begin entering formulae into our example worksheet, move the cursor to location b5 and type an equal sign (=). The equal sign indicates that a formula is about to be entered. The following message should appear at the bottom of the display:

```
FORMULA: b5=
```

The example worksheet is used to calculate the gas mileage of a vehicle based on the fact that the gas tank is filled each week. Therefore, if the week "ends" when the tank is filled, the initial mileage for the current week is the same as the final mileage for last week.

In order to perform these calculations, the values in column c should be moved down one row and over one column to the left. Therefore the formula for position b5 should simply be b5 = c4.

Type the value "c4" in response to the prompt at the bottom of the display and press Return. The value from position c4 (53521.5) will be assigned to the current cursor position (b5).

Since the formulae for positions b6 and b7 perform the same operation (with relative variables), the copy commands can be used to enter the remaining formulae in column b.

While the cursor is still located at position b5, execute the Control-w command. Proceed by moving the cursor down one line to position b6. Execute the Control-y command to recall the formula. The following message is displayed at the bottom of the display.

```
Formula: b5=>c4< Relative?
```

Notice the reversed angle brackets that are used to indicate which location should be considered relative. Press the Y key in response to the prompt and observe the results of the formula.

Since the variables have been declared (relative or non-relative) simply move the cursor down one line and execute the Control-y command. The formula takes effect immediately because the variable had been declared "Relative" in the previous step. Each of the first four columns of the worksheet should have four entries when the formulae in column b are complete.

The formulae for the last column are used to compute the miles per gallon based on the data of columns b, c and d. Column e is calculated according to the following formula.

$$\frac{\text{final mileage - initial mileage}}{\text{number of gallons}} = \text{miles per gallon}$$

In terms of the worksheet, the formula for position e4 is (c4-b4)/d4. In order to enter the formula, simply move the cursor to location e4 and type an equal sign, followed by the expression (c4-b4)/d4. When the Return key is pressed, the value 17.8 should appear in the worksheet at position e4.

When similar formulae are used in a large portion of the worksheet, a special variation of the copy commands can be used to make the task very simple.

Begin by locating the cursor at the position to be duplicated. (i.e. position e4). Execute the Control-w command and proceed by moving the cursor to the first position where you would like a copy to appear. Press the Escape key (ESC) and press the space bar. In the example worksheet, execute this command at position e5. The following message will appear at the bottom of the display:

```
Mark Set at e5
```

Once the first position has been set, move the cursor to the last location where a replica of the formula is to appear. This is location e7. Execute the Escape, y command in order to replicate the formula at positions e4 through e7. When this command is executed, the Relative prompt will appear at the bottom of the display. Since all of the variables are relative, respond to the prompt with the Y key. Then, type an exclamation mark (!) to indicate that the rest of the variables are also relative. This completes the upper part of the table. The worksheet should now appear as follows.

| | a | b | c | d | e |
|---|---|---|---|---|---|
| 1 | | Initial | Final | | |
| 2 | Date | Mileage | Mileage | Gallons | MPG |
| 3 | ---------- | ---------- | ---------- | ---------- | ---------- |
| 4 | 6-04-83 | 53347.4 | 53521.5 | 9.8 | 17.8 |
| 5 | 6-11-83 | 53521.5 | 53701.4 | 10.2 | 17.6 |
| 6 | 6-18-83 | 53701.4 | 53992.5 | 16.2 | 18.0 |
| 7 | 6-25-83 | 53992.5 | 54189.3 | 11.0 | 17.9 |
| 8 | | | | | |
| 9 | | | TOTALS | | |
| 10 | | | Miles | | |
| 11 | | | Gallons | | |
| 12 | | | MPG | | |

To calculate a value for the month's total number of miles, move the cursor to location d10 and enter the following formula.

d10= c7-b4

This formula is used to subtract the first entry in the Initial Mileage column from the last entry in the Final Mileage column. This formula should compute the value 841.9.

The value for the month's total gallons can be calculated with the sum formula. The values that are to be added are located in d4 through d7. Therefore, the value can be computed by moving the cursor to location d11 and entering the following formula.

d11=sum (d4:d7)

This formula will compute the sum of all values between positions d4 and d7. This formula should compute the value 47.2.

The final formula for the worksheet is used to calculate the overall miles per gallon for the month. This is simply the ratio of the total number of miles to the total number of gallons which can be calculated by using the following formula:

d12=d10/d11

This formula should compute the value 17.8.

All the data entry and calculation for the example worksheet are now complete. Illustration 6-2 (see page 142) depicts the values of the worksheet in its final form.

**Editing Formulae**

If a formula is entered in the worksheet incorrectly, the entry can be changed without retyping the entire formula.

To edit a formula, move the cursor to the location of the formula and execute the following command.

Control-x,e

When this command is executed, a message will be displayed at the bottom of the screen that includes the word "EDIT:", as well as the formula expression. In this mode the ← and → keys can be used to move the cursor left and right. The DEL key can be used to delete the character immediately to the left of the cursor while the Control-D command is used to delete the character in the position of the cursor. Data can be inserted into a formula simply by typing the desired information. To exit the edit mode, press the Return key.

### Locking and Unlocking Formulae

A formula can be "locked" into place to prevent it from being edited or deleted. In order to lock a formula, move the cursor to that formula position and execute the following command:

Control-x
Control-l

When a formula is locked, an "at-sign" (@) is automatically added to the formula. This character has no effect on the calculations, but is included to remind the user that the formula is locked.

A formula can be unlocked by executing the following command.

Control-x
Control-u

Formulae in an entire section of the worksheet can be locked (or unlocked) by the following procedure.

1. Move the cursor to the upper left corner of the region.
2. Press the ESC key, followed by the space bar.
3. Move the cursor to the lower right corner of the region.
4. Execute the lock (or unlock) region command.

The lock region command is Control-x,l. The unlock region command is Control-x,u.

### Deleting and Inserting Lines and Columns

There are several commands that can be used to insert and delete entries, lines, columns or regions from the worksheet. A region is defined in the same manner as described for the lock and unlock region commands.

The delete and insert commands are summarized in Table 6-5.

**Table 6-5. Delete and Insert Commands**

| | |
|---|---|
| Control-o | Insert line |
| Escape, o | Insert column |
| Control-c | Delete line |
| Escape, c | Delete column |
| Control-d | Delete entry |
| Escape,d | Delete region |

## OUTPUTTING THE WORKSHEET

The Control-x,Control-p command is used to output a copy of the worksheet without the column letters, or line numbers. When the output command is executed, the following prompt appears at the bottom of the display.

```
Print to file ⟨CR⟩ :
```

If a filename is specified, followed by the Return key, the worksheet will be written to a disk file. This allows the worksheet to be saved, printed or edited with Perfect Writer. When the Control-x,Control-p command is used to save a worksheet, it cannot be reloaded for any further calculations.

If this command was executed and no filename was specified, the worksheet will be output on the printer when the Return key is pressed.

## Saving a Worksheet

A worksheet can also be saved in a manner that allows the data to be re-used with the Perfect Calc. The Control-x, Control-s command is used to create a data file. The data file that is created will have the initial name that was specified for the Perfect Calc worksheet.

In order to reload a data file for performing more calculations, use the PC command along with the data filename in response to the system prompt. For example, if a data file is stored on the diskette in drive B, the following statement can be used to load the Perfect Calc worksheet:

A>PC B:filename.PC

It is generally a good idea to use the filename extension .PC with all Perfect Calc data files.

If you would like to save a data file, but would like to specify a filename other that the original, use the Control-x, Control-w command. This command does not automatically save the file under the current filename. When this command is executed, the following prompt will appear at the bottom of the display.

```
Write to file ⟨CR⟩ :
```

In response to this prompt, enter the filename to be used with the data file. Use the Return key to enter the name of the data file.

## Exiting Perfect Calc

The command used to exit the Perfect Calc program is Control-x, Control-c. If the worksheet currently in use has not been saved in a data file, the exit command will not automatically eliminate the worksheet. If the exit command was executed for a worksheet that had been modified since the last time it was saved the following prompt will be displayed.

```
Ignore changes this session?
```

If the response to this prompt is Y, the modifications of the worksheet will be ignored, a warm boot will be executed, and the system prompt will be displayed. If the response to the prompt is N, the program is not exited and the normal worksheet operations resume.

## Help

When the Perfect Calc program is executing, a list of possible commands can be displayed at any time by entering the question mark (?) command.

When the question mark is executed, a list of 16 general categories will be displayed at the bottom of the monitor. When a value from 1 through 16 is entered, a list of commands that deal with the specified topic will be displayed.

For example, after the question mark has been entered, selection number 3 on the menu will appear as "Entering data and formulas". In order to display the commands used to enter data and formulae, type the number 3 followed by the Return key.

## MULTIPLE WORKSHEETS

The Perfect Calc program allows up to seven worksheets to be active at the same time. The commands used to create and access multiple buffers with the Perfect Calc program are exactly the same as the commands used with the Perfect Writer program. A complete explanation of the use of multiple buffers is contained in Chapter 3, on pages 62-64.

The commands (and associated prompts) that are used to manipulate buffers are listed in Table 6-6.

**Table 6-6. Multiple Buffer Commands and Prompts**

| Command | Prompt | Action |
|---|---|---|
| Control-x,Control-f | File to find 〈CR〉: | Create a buffer for the specified file. |
| Control-x,b | Switch to Buffer 〈CR〉: | Switch to specified buffer. |
| Control-x,k | Delete Buffer 〈CR〉: | Delete the specified buffer. |
| Control-x,Control-b | | Display list of active buffers. |

## Split Screen Worksheet

The Perfect Calc program allows two worksheets to be displayed on the screen at the same time. The program also allows values or entire regions to be copied from one worksheet onto another using the same procedures described earlier.

A split screen display can contain two worksheets side by side, or one on top of the other. The worksheets can also be synchronized so that the same columns (or lines) from the two worksheets will be displayed adjacent to each other.

To create a split screen display with two vertical worksheets (side by side), move the cursor to the column where you would like the second worksheet to begin. Move the cursor up to row number 1 and execute the Control-x,2 command.

To create a split screen display with two horizontal worksheets (one on top of the other), move the cursor to the row where you would like the second worksheet to begin. Move the cursor to column a and execute the Control-x,2 command.

When the split screen command has been executed, the following prompt will be displayed:

```
Synchronize windows?
```

This prompt requires either a Y or N response. If the Y selection is chosen, the same columns or rows of the two worksheets will always be displayed simultaneously.

Two side by side synchronized worksheets will always have the same row numbers displayed. Similarly, two worksheets that are on top of each other and synchronized will share the same columns.

In other words, synchronized worksheets automatically move together and unsynchronized worksheets can be moved independently.

For example, consider a split screen display that contains two worksheets, side by side. If the two worksheets are synchronized, each row of the left worksheet appears next to the corresponding row in the right worksheet. Row number 1 on the left appears next to row number 1 on the right. If the cursor in the worksheet on the right is moved to row number 100, the left worksheet automatically moves to the same position.

If the two worksheets were not synchronized, the left worksheet would not automatically move to follow the worksheet on the right, or vice versa.

Once a split screen display has been created, a second worksheet can be displayed by executing the Control-x, Control-f command. This command displays the "File to find" prompt. Be sure to specify a Perfect Calc data file in response to this prompt.

All of the multiple buffer commands described earlier can be used in the same way when split screen worksheets are in effect.

Table 6-7 provides a summary of the commands that are used to manipulate split screen displays.

**Table 6-7. Split Screen Display Commands**

| | |
|---|---|
| Control-x,2 | Create split screen display. |
| Control-x,1 | Return to single worksheet display. |
| Control-x,o | Move the cursor to the other worksheet. |
| Control-x, Control-v | Move the other window down one page. |
| Control-x, Control-z | Move the other window up one page. |
| Control-x,v | Move the other window one page right. |
| Control-x,z | Move the other window one page left. |

This chapter does not contain a complete explanation of all the subtle features of the Perfect Calc program. Please consult the **Perfect Calc User's Guide** for any further details.

# CHAPTER 7.
# PROFIT PLAN

## INTRODUCTION

Profit Plan is an applications program developed by Chang Laboratories. Profit Plan is used to solve planning problems, and to produce various types of charts and tables. Profit Plan is basically a worksheet, similar to Perfect Calc. However, the Profit Plan program has provisions for generating reports. Profit Plan is provided as part of the standard software package for the Kaypro computer.

### Getting Started

The Profit Plan master diskette should be promptly copied and placed in a safe place. Also, the "working copy" of the diskette should contain a copy of the operating system. Chapter 2 contains an explanation of the FORMAT, COPY and SYSGEN commands needed to generate a working copy of the master Profit Plan diskette.

Begin by turning on the power of the computer and inserting the working copy of the Profit Plan diskette into disk drive A. The computer should "start up" and display the message:

```
KAYPRO II
64k CP/M v 2.2

A>
```

If a different message is displayed on the screen (i.e. Hello there...), the diskette does not contain a copy of the operating system. If this is the case, be sure that you are using a *copy* of the master Profit Plan diskette, then use the SYSGEN command to copy the operating system.

When the system prompt (A>) appears, respond by typing PP, followed by pressing the Return key.

A>PP

When this command is entered, the disk drive begins to operate, and a copyright message is displayed, followed by a vendor code and the diskette registration number.

Following these messages, the Profit Plan worksheet is displayed (see Illustration 7-1). This worksheet is used to solve problems using the Profit Plan program.

If it is necessary to return to CP/M, simply press the reset switch on the back of the main computer console.

## Concept

The main concept behind the Profit Plan program is the use of the organized format of the worksheet to set up financial (or any other type) of calculations. The program calculates the values in the table according to a set of instructions specified by the user.

An important feature of the Profit Plan program is the ability to generate charts and tables. Even if no calculations are necessary, the format of the worksheet makes Profit Plan convenient for generating reports.

## Configuration

The worksheet can be used to manipulate up to 1000 items of data. The worksheet is arranged in 50 rows and 20 columns, although the entire worksheet need not be used.

**Illustration 7-1. Original Worksheet Format**

```
                                 MODE=NORMAL  ORDER=R/C  ROW=1-50  COL=1-20
  ROW 1
ENTER COMMAND:
                                                                       1  FORMAT:
  ROW                                                                  2  DATA:
  -----      ----1----   ----2----   ----3----   ----4----   ----5---- 3  MATH:
    1            0.0         0.0         0.0         0.0         0.0   4  PRINT:
    2            0.0         0.0         0.0         0.0         0.0   5  UTILITY:
    3            0.0         0.0         0.0         0.0         0.0   6  COMPUTE
    4            0.0         0.0         0.0         0.0         0.0   7  HELP
    5            0.0         0.0         0.0         0.0         0.0   8
    6            0.0         0.0         0.0         0.0         0.0   9  STOP
    7            0.0         0.0         0.0         0.0         0.0   10 ROW RANGE
    8            0.0         0.0         0.0         0.0         0.0   11 COL RANGE
    9            0.0         0.0         0.0         0.0         0.0   12 ORDER
   10            0.0         0.0         0.0         0.0         0.0   13 SET DRIVE
   11            0.0         0.0         0.0         0.0         0.0   14 SET UP
   12            0.0         0.0         0.0         0.0         0.0   15 SET CRT
   13            0.0         0.0         0.0         0.0         0.0   16
   14            0.0         0.0         0.0         0.0         0.0   17
   15            0.0         0.0         0.0         0.0         0.0   18 FORMAT:
   16            0.0         0.0         0.0         0.0         0.0   19    ROWS:
   17            0.0         0.0         0.0         0.0         0.0   20 ROW TITLE
```

Each column and row of the worksheet can be given a title. Also, the worksheet itself can be given a title. A typical example of a finished worksheet is provided in Illustration 7-2.

This chapter provides a complete explanation of the procedure needed to produce the worksheet depicted in Illustration 7-2.

The first step in producing the worksheet is setting the column and row titles. The second step is the entering of data. The third step is performing the mathematic calculations. Two different methods of calculating the values on the worksheet are demonstrated.

The discussion prodeeds with the method used to recalculate the worksheet for a different set of data. The final procedure in producing the worksheet is setting the titles and determining the style of the output.

The final section of the chapter describes the procedure used to output the worksheet on a printer. This section also includes some of the commands that are used for general operations of the program.

Profit Plan is particularly useful in performing calculations on a large number of sets of data. Financial data from a number of years, sales records for a number of salespersons, or results from the same experiment repeated many times, are all excellent applications for the Profit Plan program. The program is also convenient for forecasting situations, given a standard means of analysis.

**Display**

The majority of the display is occupied with the worksheet. However there are several other important areas on the display.

The right edge of the screen is reserved for a listing of the commands used with the Profit Plan program.

**Illustration 7-2. Typical Application of Profit Plan**

SALES REPORT
FIRST QUARTER
1983

| | JOHN STEVENS | TOM SALEM | JIM THOMSON | BOB HOWARD | TOTAL |
|---|---|---|---|---|---|
| JANUARY | $237.89 | $334.97 | $453.77 | $543.23 | $1,569.86 |
| FEBRUARY | $241.99 | $302.89 | $402.64 | $520.88 | $1,468.40 |
| MARCH | $200.87 | $305.99 | $430.90 | $498.43 | $1,436.19 |
| TOTAL SALES | $680.75 | $943.85 | $1,287.31 | $1,562.54 | $4,474.45 |
| QUOTA | $600.00 | $900.00 | $1,200.00 | $1,500.00 | $4,200.00 |
| % ABOVE QUOTA | 13.46% | 4.87% | 7.28% | 4.17% | 6.53% |

THOUSANDS OF DOLLARS

The prompt that appears near the upper-left corner of the screen:

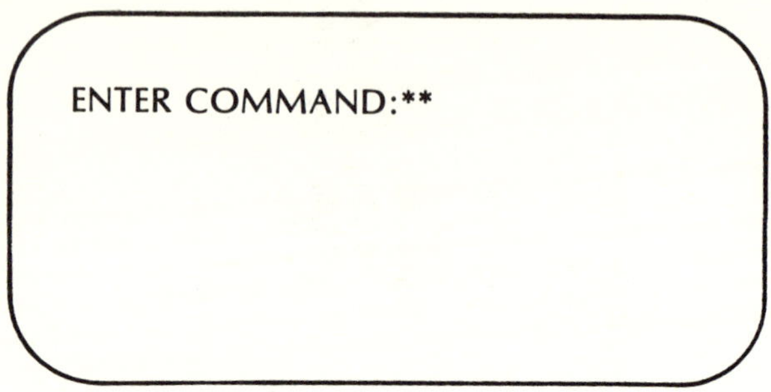


indicates that the program is ready to accept a command. The number of the command that is chosen appears where the asterisks (**) appear in the prompt.

The area on the screen immediately to the right of the prompt and above the worksheet is reserved to display special instructions.

## COMMANDS

The commands used in the Profit Plan program belong to five major categories. These categories, FORMAT, DATA, MATH, PRINT and UTILITY each contain several commands.

These commands are used to set up the worksheet, enter data, manipulate the data, and output the results. The commands are also used to perform other miscellaneous functions.

The list of commands on the right side of the display contain only 5 entries that are followed by a colon (:). The original configuration of the command area of the display is depicted in Illustration 7-3.

**Illustration 7-3. The Command Area**

| | |
|---|---|
| 1 | FORMAT: |
| 2 | DATA: |
| 3 | MATH: |
| 4 | PRINT: |
| 5 | UTILITY: |
| 6 | COMPUTE |
| 7 | HELP |
| 8 | |
| 9 | STOP |
| 10 | ROW RANGE |
| 11 | COL RANGE |
| 12 | ORDER |
| 13 | SET DRIVE |
| 14 | SET UP |
| 15 | SET CRT |
| 16 | |
| 17 | |
| 18 | FORMAT: |
| 19 | ROWS: |
| 20 | ROW TITLE |

The first five entries on the menu represent the five main categories: FORMAT, DATA, MATH, PRINT and UTILITY. The commands 1 through 5 cause the menu to change to the list of commands in the specified category. For example, since command number 3 is MATH:, when command number 3 is executed, the list of MATH commands (ADD, SUBTRACT...) appear in the menu area (see Illustration 7-4).

**Illustration 7-4. The MATH Commands**

| | |
|---|---|
| 40 | MATH: |
| 41 | ADD |
| 42 | SUBTRACT |
| 43 | MULTIPLY |
| 44 | DIVIDE |
| 45 | NEGATE |
| 46 | INVERSE |
| 47 | INTEGER |
| 48 | ROUND |
| 49 | CUMULATE |
| 50 | ABSOLUTE |
| 51 | ADD K |
| 52 | SUB K |
| 53 | MULT K |
| 54 | DIV K |
| 55 | SUM |
| 56 | GET |
| 57 | FLOOR |
| 58 | CEILING |
| 59 | |

## Prompt

The Profit Plan program uses a pair of square brackets ([ ]) to indicate the position on the worksheet where the next data item will appear. This prompt is not only used for the values on the table, but for the row and column titles as well.

The prompt surrounds a value in the table when the ENTER* command is active. When any other commands are active, the prompt will surround a row or column heading. When the Profit Plan program is performing operations on a row or a column, the prompt appears in the heading of the row or column that is affected by the command.

---

* The ENTER command is used to enter data in the table. This command will be discussed later in this chapter.

When a command is performed, the prompt automatically moves to the next position. However, the ↑ and ↓ keys can be used to change the row of the prompt. Similarly, the ← and → keys are used to change the column.

When the ENTER command is active, the prompt can be moved to any location in the table with the "arrow" keys.

The prompt can be moved from the row heading area to the column heading area by executing a SELECT COL command. The prompt can be moved back to the row heading area with the SELECT ROW command. These two commands are discussed in depth later in this chapter.

**Errors**

Generally, the errors made in the Profit Plan program are very easy to correct.

If you realize that you typed an incorrect value before the data is actually entered*, simply use the BACKSPACE key to back up over the mistake.

If an incorrect command was entered, but the actual operation of the command was not executed, press the DEL key to exit the command.

For example, if command number 31 (ENTER DATA) was executed by mistake, but no data was actually entered, press the DEL key to cancel the command.

If an incorrect command was executed, and the operation actually took effect, simply repeat the command with the correct instructions. When mistakes are being corrected, be sure that the prompt is in the correct location. The prompt always moves to the next location when a command is executed. As a result, it generally is necessary to move the prompt back to the original line.

---

* The data that is typed on the keyboard is not actually entered until the Return key is pressed.

For example, if the row title "FEBRUARY" is entered for a row instead of "JANUARY", simply move the prompt back to the row that contains the error and repeat the command with the correct value.

## FORMAT COMMANDS

In response to the prompt:

ENTER COMMAND:**

enter 1 followed by pressing the Return key.

ENTER COMMAND:1*

The result of this command is that the list of FORMAT commands will appear on the menu.

The only two FORMAT commands that are generally of interest are number 20, ROW TITLE and 25, COL TITLE. The rest of the FORMAT commands are described in the final section of this chapter.

Command 20 is used to label the rows of the worksheet, while command 25 is used to lable the columns. The preceeding example (Illustration 7-2) contains the row labels JANUARY, FEBRUARY, etc. These titles can be generated with the following procedure.

Enter command number 20, followed by pressing the Return key. Enter the word JANUARY followed by the Return key. The title for the first row is now JANUARY.

Notice the square brackets ( [ ] ) at row number 2. These brackets indicate that the next title will be assigned to row number 2. The cursor up ( ↑ ) and cursor down ( ↓ ) keys can be used to move the square brackets to another row. The brackets automatically move down one row with each entry of a title.

Proceed by entering FEBRUARY, followed by Return. When a complete set of row labels have been entered, press the DEL key to proceed with another command.

Even though the entire row title may not appear on the worksheet, the complete name is included in the final output.

The COL TITLE command is used in a similar manner to the ROW TITLE command. However, each column title can consist of two entries. In the example in Illustration 7-2, each name contains a single entry.

To begin labeling the column, enter command 25 followed by Return. The prompt line appears as follows:

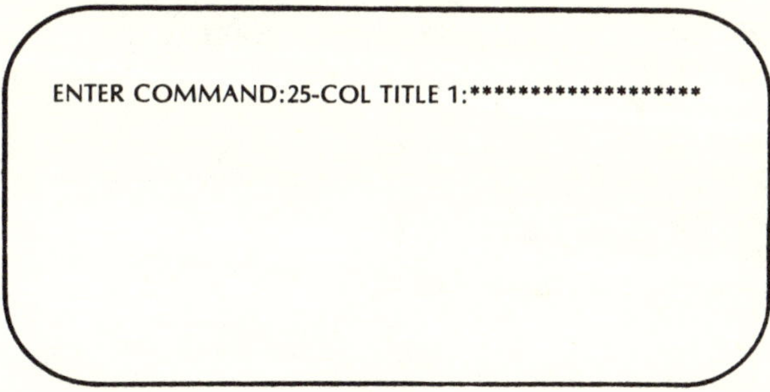


Enter the desired column title for column 1 (for example: JOHN STEVENS). When the Return key is pressed, another prompt appears on the display.

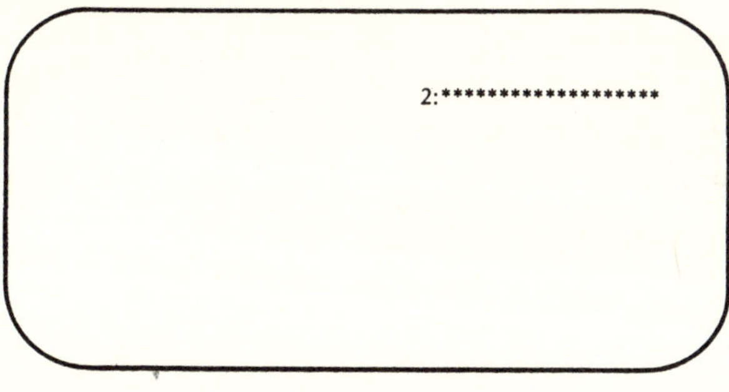

Enter the second title in response to this prompt. If only one title is desired (as in the example), simply press the Return key in response to this prompt.

Once again, only a token of the title appears on the display. The cursor control keys ← and → can be used to move the square brackets to another column. The next column titles are assigned to the column where the square brackets are located. When all the column titles have been entered, press the DEL key.

The column and row labels can be entered onto the worksheet by entering the following data at the keyboard.

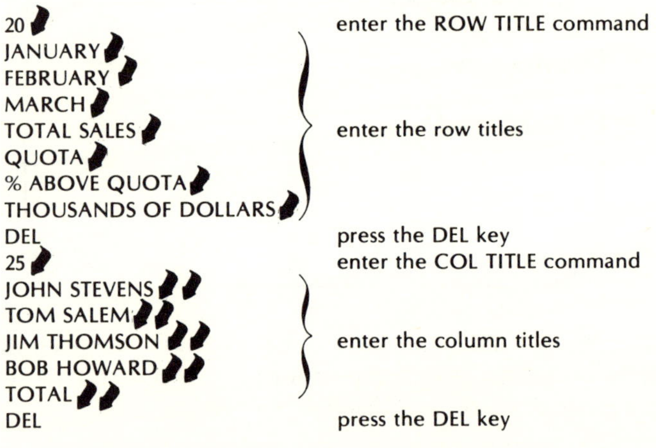

20 — enter the ROW TITLE command
JANUARY
FEBRUARY
MARCH
TOTAL SALES
QUOTA
% ABOVE QUOTA
THOUSANDS OF DOLLARS
enter the row titles
DEL — press the DEL key
25 — enter the COL TITLE command
JOHN STEVENS
TOM SALEM
JIM THOMSON
BOB HOWARD
TOTAL
enter the column titles
DEL — press the DEL key


When the column and row headings are entered, the table will appear as follows:

| ROW | JOHN STEV | TOM SALEM | JIM THOMS | BOB HOWAR | TOTAL |
|---|---|---|---|---|---|
| ------- | ---------1--------- | ---------2--------- | ---------3--------- | ---------4--------- | ---------5--------- |
| [ 1 JANUARY ] | 0.0 | 0.0 | 0.0 | 0.0 | 0.0 |
| 2 FEBRUARY | 0.0 | 0.0 | 0.0 | 0.0 | 0.0 |
| 3 MARCH | 0.0 | 0.0 | 0.0 | 0.0 | 0.0 |
| 4 TOTAL SALES | 0.0 | 0.0 | 0.0 | 0.0 | 0.0 |
| 5 QUOTA | 0.0 | 0.0 | 0.0 | 0.0 | 0.0 |
| 6 % ABOVE QUOT | 0.0 | 0.0 | 0.0 | 0.0 | 0.0 |
| 7 THOUSANDS OF | 0.0 | 0.0 | 0.0 | 0.0 | 0.0 |

The rest of the table headings are blank.

**DATA**

The commands that are commonly used to enter data on the table are ENTER, CHANGE, SELECT ROW, SELECT COL and FORMULA. The data that is entered can be organized either in rows or columns. Generally, the data is organized in rows because the columns all describe a similar item (years, salesmen, etc.).

The list of DATA commands can be displayed on the menu by executing command number 2.

Command number 31 is the ENTER command. This command can be used to enter data in any of four modes. Data can be entered as individual values, constant values, numbers with a constant rate of growth, or numbers with a constant rate of increase.

For example the data:

237.89 543.23 453.77 334.97

would have to be entered as inidividual values, because there are no relationships between the values.

The data:

100 100 100 100

could be entered as a constant value.

The data:

200 300 450 675

could be entered as data with a constant rate of growth. Notice that each number increases by 50%. As a result, the base value, or initial value of this data is 200, and the rate of growth is 50%.

The data:

200 250 300 350

could be entered as data with a constant rate of increase. The base value in this case is 200, and the rate of increase is 50.

The square brackets are used to indicate where the data will appear on the table. If the brackets enclose a row heading, the data will be entered at that row. To select a different row, use the cursor up ( ↑ ) and cursor down ( ↓ ) keys.

If you wish to enter the data in a column, execute command number 34 (SELECT COL) to move the brackets to a column heading. Use the cursor left (←) and cursor right (→) keys to move the square brackets to the desired column heading.

The four types of data can be entered with the ENTER command (number 31). When this command is executed, the prompt line appears as follows:

CHOOSE (VALUES=0,CONSTANT=1,GROW=1,INCR=3):*

The values 0, 1, 2, and 3 are used to select individual values, constants, data with constant growth or data with constant increase.

To enter the data into the table in Illustration 7-2 make the following entries at the keyboard.

| | |
|---|---|
| 31↵ | execute ENTER command |
| 0↵ | select individual values |
| 237.89↵<br>334.97↵<br>453.77↵<br>543.23↵ | enter first row data |
| ←←←←↓ | move the brackets to the first position of the second row. |

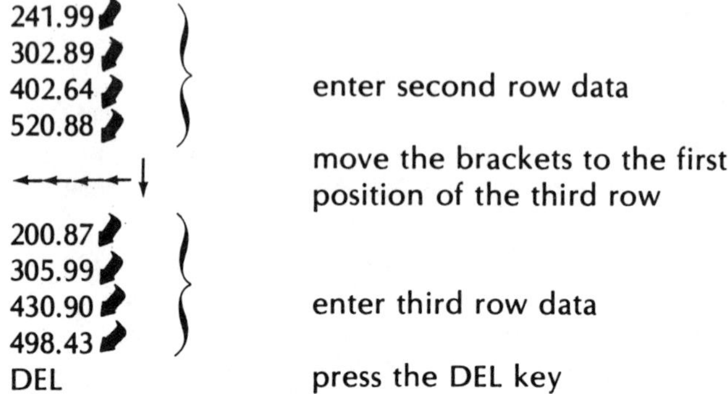


The data for the QUOTA (row 5) consists of numbers with a constant rate of increase. As a result, these values can be entered in one step. Make the following entries to enter the QUOTA data.

| | |
|---|---|
| 33 | execute the SELECT ROW command |
| 5 | select row 5 (QUOTA) |
| 31 | execute the ENTER command |
| 3 | choose data with constant increase |
| 600 | choose a base value of 600 |
| 300 | choose a rate of increase of 300 |

The data entry to the table is now complete. The rest of the values on the table can be calculated by the Profit Plan program. The table should now appear as follows.

| ROW | JOHN STEV | TOM SALEM | JIM THOMS | BOB HOWAR | TOTAL |
|---|---|---|---|---|---|
| ------- | ---------1--------- | ---------2--------- | ---------3--------- | ---------4--------- | ---------5--------- |
| 1 JANUARY | 237.9 | 335.0 | 453.8 | 543.2 | 0.0 |
| 2 FEBRUARY | 242.0 | 302.9 | 402.6 | 520.9 | 0.0 |
| 3 MARCH | 200.9 | 306.0 | 430.9 | 498.4 | 0.0 |
| 4 TOTAL SALES | 0.0 | 0.0 | 0.0 | 0.0 | 0.0 |
| 5 QUOTA | 600.0 | 900.0 | 1,200.0 | 1,500.0 | 1,800.0 |
| [ 6 % ABOVE QUOT ] | 0.0 | 0.0 | 0.0 | 0.0 | 0.0 |
| 7 THOUSANDS OF | | | | | |

The entries do not appear exactly as they are entered, but the correct values appear in the final output. The value 1,800.0 is not the correct value for the total QUOTA, but this value will be changed later.

## MATH

The list of MATH commands can be displayed in the menu area by executing command number 3. Commands 41 through 44, ADD, SUBTRACT, MULTIPLY and DIVIDE are used to perform the associated mathematical operation between the rows (or columns) of the table.

Commands 51 through 54 are used to perform the same mathematical operations between a row (or column) of the table and a constant value.

To provide the values for row 4 on the table, the SUM command is used to add up the values in the first 3 rows. Before the numbers are added, the SELECT ROW command is used to make the values appear in row 4. The following entries are used to derive the values for row 4.

| | |
|---|---|
| 33 | execute the SELECT ROW command |
| 4 | select row 4 |
| 55 | execute the SUM command |
| 1 | specify the first row to be added |
| 3 | specify the last row to be added |

The values:

680.8 943.9 1,287.3 1,562.5

should appear now in row 4 of the table.

The SUM command is also used to calculate the totals for column 5. The SELECT COL command (number 34) is used to specify the location for the values. The SUM command (number 55) is executed to compute the totals. The values 1 and 4 are used to specify the first and last columns that are added together. The following entries are used to compute the values for column 5.

| | |
|---|---|
| 34 | execute SELECT COL command |
| 5 | choose column 5 |
| 55 | execute SUM command |
| 1 | specify the first column in the sum |
| 4 | specify the last column in the sum |

The table should appear as follows.

| ROW | JOHN STEV | TOM SALEM | JIM THOMS | BOB HOWAR | TOTAL |
|---|---|---|---|---|---|
| ------- | ---------1--------- | ---------2--------- | ---------3-------- | ---------4--------- | ---------5--------- |
| 1 JANUARY | 237.9 | 335.0 | 453.8. | 54.2 | 1,569.9 |
| 2 FEBRUARY | 242.0 | 302.9 | 402.6 | 520.9 | 1,468.4 |
| 3 MARCH | 200.9 | 306.0 | 430.9 | 498.4 | 1,436.2 |
| 4 TOTAL SALES | 680.8 | 943.9 | 1,287.3 | 1,562.5 | 4,474.5 |
| 5 QUOTA | 600.0 | 900.0 | 1,200.0 | 1,500.0 | 4,200.0 |
| 6 % ABOVE QUOT | 0.0 | 0.0 | 0.0 | 0.0 | 0.0 |
| 7 THOUSANDS OF | 0.0 | 0.0 | 0.0 | 0.0 | 0.0 |

Calculating row 6 of the table requires the use of a formula. The FORMULA command is not actually a MATH command, it is a DATA command (number 35).

A formula can contain the operators + - * and / to represent addition, subtraction, multiplication and division. If the operations are performed for a row of the table, any other row of the table can be specified by the letter L and the row number.

For example, if a row of values is to be calculated by the formula L1 + L2 + L4 - L3, the results will be the values of row 3 subtracted from the sum of rows 1, 2 and 4. If a column of values is to be calculated, the same formula will represent the sum of columns 1, 2 and 4 minus the values in column 3.

If a particular value from the table is needed in a calculation, the value can be specified by the letter V followed by the row and column numbers, separated by a comma.

For example, in a formula, the value V2,1 represents the value in row 2, column 1.

The following example formulae all have the correct format.

L1 + L2 - L4 + 128
L1/L2 + (L1 * L2)
(L1 + L2 + L6)/10

Multiplication and division are performed before addition and subtraction in a formula.

Unfortunately, negative numbers cannot be used in a formula. The number -250 must be represent in the form (0 - 250).

The formula needed to determine the percent above or below the quota is as follows:

$$\frac{\text{line 4 - line 5}}{\text{line 5}} \times 100$$

In order for the formula to be used with command number 35, it must take on the following form.

(L4 - L5)/L5 * 100

As a result, row 6 of the table can be calculated by making the following entries.

| | |
|---|---|
| 33 | execute SELECT ROW command |
| 6 | specify row number 6 |
| 35 | execute the FORMULA command |
| (L4 — L5)/L5 * 100 | enter the formula |

The entire table of values is now complete.

**Compute**

Another feature of the Profit Plan program is the ability to recalculate the table after changing one or several items of data.

For example, consider the possibility that JOHN STEVENS' sales were 1237.89 in JANUARY instead of 237.89. To change this value, execute the CHANGE command (number 32) as follows.

| | |
|---|---|
| 32 | execute CHANGE command |
| 1 | specify row 1 |
| 1 | specify column 1 |
| 1237.89 | specify the new value |

When the new value is added, the results of the table remain the same. However, when the COMPUTE command (number 6) is executed, the entire table will be recalculated with the new value.

**CAUTION**

Using the COMPUTE command does not necessarily preserve the order in which the operations were performed. Notice that the table does not return to its original form when the original data is re-entered.

Recall the order that the operations were originally performed. The values in column 5 were calculated before the values in row 6. However, the COMPUTE command performs all the operations on the rows before the operations on the columns. This is a different order from that in which they were originally performed.

The total percent above quota was calculated to be 6.5% originally. However, the COMPUTE command returns the value 29.8%. The difference between these values is that 6.5% is the *percent of the sums* while 29.8% is the *sum of the percents.* This is a subtle mathematical difference, but the results are very significant. Avoid using the COMPUTE command unless you are sure that the program will perform operations in the same order as was originally intended, unless the order of the operations will not affect the results of the calculations.

The message ORDER=R/C is displayed at the top of the screen to remind the operator that the rows are calculated before the columns. Command number 12 is used to specify the order of the operations. When the ORDER command is executed, a selection of 4 items will be presented. Selection number one specifies that only the row operations are executed. Selection number two specifies that only the column operations are executed.

The third selection indicates that the rows are calculated before the columns, and the fourth selection indicates that the columns are calculated before the rows.

## PRINTING REPORTS

There are four commands that are used in printing reports. These commands are SET TYPE (rows), SET TYPE (columns), OPTIONS and TITLES.

The SET TYPE commands are used to set the basic format of the data in the table. The OPTIONS command is used to set the parameters of the output. The TITLES command is used to set up the headings of the table. These four commands are used to produce a report with the values that are calculated in the worksheet.

### SET TYPE

Command number 21 is the SET TYPE command for rows. When this command is executed, six prompts will appear. The initial prompt is for the row number which is to be formatted. The remaining five prompts specify the style of the output for that row. Each of these prompts are listed in Table 7-1 along with its default value and possible options for the prompt.

When a prompt message is displayed, note the CURRENT= message that is also displayed in the upper right hand corner of the screen. The value indicated by CURRENT= is the prompt option that was specified the last time SET TYPE was executed. If SET TYPE had not been previously executed, the CURRENT= will be the default value (see Table 7-1).

After the SET TYPE command has been executed, the Row prompt will appear. The user must key in a row value (1-50). When this has been completed, each parameter will be prompted for an entry at the top of the display.

**Table 7-1. SET TYPE Prompts and Default Values for Rows**

| prompt | prompt options | default |
|---|---|---|
| ROW | 1 through 50 | no default |
| TYPE | DATA, SUBTITLE, HEADING, NOTE, OMIT | DATA |
| UNDERLINE | NONE, DASH(-), EQUAL(=), STARS(*) | NONE |
| TRAILING BLANK LINES | 0 through 8, NEW PAGE | 0 |
| DECIMAL PLACES | 0 through 3 | 1 |
| FORMAT | OFF, PERCENT(%), DOLLAR SIGN($) | OFF |

After an entry has been made for the Row prompt, the second prompt will appear. This prompt requests the type of information occupying the specified row. Generally, selection O (DATA) is specified. However, other selections are available for subtitles, headings, footnotes and omitting a line.

Subtitles, headings and footnotes are used to insert text into the final output. These parameters allow words to be placed in the table instead of numeric values.

The omit parameter allows an entire row of the worksheet to be left out of the final output table.

The third prompt asks the user whether he wishes the specified row to be underlined. Either stars, dashes or equal signs can be used to underline a row of output. In our example, Rows 1 through 6 are not underlined, row 7 is underlined with dashes.

The fourth prompt asks for the number of blank lines that follow a row of output. None of the rows in the example contain trailing blank lines. If selection number 9 is chosen, the table will begin a new page after the specified row.

The fifth prompt asks for the number of decimal places. Rows 1 through 6 in the example have 2 decimal places.

Since row number 7 contains a comment instead of numeric data, the number of decimal places for row 7 has no effect on the output.

The last prompt asks if the data should be preceded by a dollar sign or followed by a percent sign. Lines 1 through 5 have a preceeding dollar sign, and line 6 has a following percent sign. This value also has no effect on the output for row 7 because the dollar sign and percent sign are only used with numeric values.

The effects of the SET TYPE command are not actually visible on the monitor. The selections of this command are only used to set the style of the output table.

The SET TYPE values for the example are summarized in Table 7-2.

When the SET TYPE information for one row has been completed, the prompt automatically asks for another row number. When all the data has been entered, press the DEL key in response to the ROW prompt. If the DEL key is pressed at any other time, the information that was entered will be lost!

The SET TYPE command for columns (26) is similar to the SET TYPE command for rows, but there are only 3 parameters to set. These 3 categories: column width, decimal places and format, are generally used when the worksheet is organized in columns instead of rows. Since the data in the example is arranged in rows, it is not necessary to execute the SET TYPE command for columns.

If specifications are provided for the columns and rows simultaneously, the specifications for columns take precedence over the row specifications.

For example, the SET TYPE commands can be used to include a percent sign with the values in column 1 and a dollar sign with the values in row 1. In this case, the value in row 1, column 1 will be assigned *both* a dollar sign *and* a percent sign. Since the column definitions take precedence, the value is actually displayed with a percent sign only.

Table 7-3 includes the prompts and default values of the SET TYPE command for columns.

**Table 7-2. SET TYPE Values for the Example Report**

| | TYPE | UNDERLINE | BLANK LINES | DECIMAL PLACES | FORMAT |
|---|---|---|---|---|---|
| rows 1 through 5 | 0 | 0 | 0 | 2 | 2 |
| row 6 | 0 | 0 | 0 | 2 | 1 |
| row 7 | 1 | 1 | 0 | X | X |

X=doesn't matter

**Table 7-3. SET TYPE Parameters and Default Values for Columns**

| prompt | prompt options | default |
|---|---|---|
| ROW | 1 through 20 | no default |
| COLUMN WIDTH | 4 through 20 spaces | 10 |
| DECIMAL PLACES | 0 through 3 | 1 |
| FORMAT | OFF, PERCENT(%), DOLLAR SIGN($) | OFF |

**OPTIONS (Command 71)**

Command number 71 is the OPTIONS command. When this command is executed, twelve parameters for the style of the output are to be selected. Each of these parameters is summarized in Table 7-4 along with its default value.

When the OPTIONS command is executed, each prompt appears near the top of the monitor, along with the prompt options.

```
MODE=NORMAL ORDER=R/C ROW=1-50  COL=1-20
ROW 1                         CURRENT=20
           ROW DESCRIPTION WIDTH (4-40)**
```

The list of choices is displayed, as well as the current value. If the current value is satisfactory, simply press the Return key. The OPTIONS command automatically proceeds through the list of prompts.

The first prompt asks for the width of the row description titles. This value should be at least as large as the number of characters in the largest row description. In the example, the row description for row 6 is 13 characters long. Since row number 7 contains a subtitle, the length of the row description at line 7 is not pertinent. As a result, the row description width is set to 13.

The second prompt asks for the width of the columns. Since the column title for column number 3 is 11 characters long, a convenient column width would be 13 characters.

**Table 7-4. OPTIONS Parameters and Default Values**

| prompt | prompt options | default |
|---|---|---|
| ROW DESCRIPTION WIDTH | 4 through 40 spaces | 20 |
| COLUMN WIDTH | 4 through 20 spaces | 10 |
| NUMBER OF COLUMNS PER PAGE | 1 through 20 | 10 |
| NUMBER OF DECIMAL PLACES | 0 through 3 | 1 |
| OMIT ZERO ROWS | NO, YES | NO |
| SUPRESS ZERO VALUES | NO, DASH, BLANK | NO |
| PRINT ROW DESC AFTER WHICH COLUMN | 0 through 9 | 0 |
| NEGATIVE NUMBERS | Preceding minus, following minus, parenthesis | Preceding minus |
| PAGE CONTROL | OFF, FORM FEED, PAUSE | OFF |
| OMIT COMMAS | NO, YES | NO |
| DOUBLS SPACE | NO, YES | NO |
| OMIT LINE NUMBERS | NO, YES | NO |

The third prompt asks for the number of columns in the table. The example contains 5 columns. Note that the column of row titles is not considered a column of the table. The "number of columns" prompt refers to numeric values only.

The fourth prompt asks for the number of decimal places. Since none of the data items in the example contain more than 2 decimal places, the value 2 is entered in response to this prompt.

The fifth prompt asks if rows that have only zeros should be deleted from the table. When a row of the table contains no data (except zeroes) it is usually convenient to leave the entire row out of the finished table. The OMIT ZERO ROWS command is used to exclude rows that contain only zeroes as data.

The sixth prompt asks if zeroes should be replaced with dashes or blank spaces. In some situations, it is convenient to replace zero values with a dash, or leave them out completely.

The seventh prompt asks if the row descriptions should appear at the left side of the page, or alternatively between the columns of data. If any value other than zero is chosen, some of the data appears to the left of the row descriptions.

The eighth prompt asks for the format of negative numbers. Numbers less than zero can be preceded by a minus sign, followed by a minus sign, or enclosed in parentheses.

The ninth prompt asks if the output should pause at the end of a page, proceed to a new page (FF) or continue without regard for the end of the page. If your printer only accepts one sheet of paper at a time, use the PAUSE selection. If your printer uses continuous paper, use the FORM FEED option.

The tenth prompt asks if the values output in the table should include commas. When commas are included, the value ten thousand would appear as 10,000. However, if commas are not included, the same value would appear as 10000.

The eleventh prompt asks if the output should be double spaced.

The twelfth prompt asks if the line numbers at the left of the page should be deleted. These are the numbers used to identify the rows of the table. These values can either be included in or deleted from the final table.

If the Return key is used as a response to a prompt, the specification remains the same as its original value. Also, it is not necessary to execute the OPTIONS command if the specifications of the table remain the same. Once the OPTIONS command has been executed, OPTIONS need only be executed again if some change in the format of the output is desired.

Every table that is output has the specifications that were chosen in the last OPTIONS command. If an OPTIONS command was not executed, each table is output according to the default parameters.

**TITLES (Command 72)**

The last command that is required to generate an output table is the TITLES command (number 72). The format of this command is the same as the OPTIONS command. Each prompt is followed by the prompt options, as well as the current values. The prompts of the TITLES command are summarized in Table 7-5.

**Table 7-5. TITLES Parameters and Default Values**

| prompt | prompt options | default |
|---|---|---|
| PAGE NUMBER | 1 through 999, NONE | NONE |
| DATE | 01 through 99, NONE | NONE |
| MONTH | 1 through 12, NONE | NONE |
| DAY | 1 through 31, NONE | NONE |
| ROW-RANGE BEGIN/END | 1 through 50 | no default |
| COL-RANGE BEGIN/END | 1 through 20 | no default |
| TITLE 1 | 0 through 40 character title | NONE |
| TITLE 2 | 0 through 40 character title | NONE |
| TITLE 3 | 0 through 40 character title | NONE |

The first option of the TITLES command is the page number. Any page number from 1 through 999 can be printed on the output. However, when a value of 0 is specified, no page number appears on the output.

The second option is the date. The year, month and day are entered as numbers. If zero is specified for the year, no date appears on the output.

The third option is the range of rows that are to appear in the output.

The fourth option is the range of columns that are to appear in the output.

The last option is the title of the output table. The title can consist of three lines, each with a maximum of 40 characters.

After the third line of the title has been entered, the output is ready to be printed. Be sure that the printer is turned on and ready to operate. Proceed by pressing the Return key. The printer will immediately begin printing the output.

The TITLES command is similar to the OPTIONS command in that once it has been executed, it need only be executed again in order to make changes in the format of the output.

## UTILITY

The UTILITY commands are generally used to store tables on a diskette, load tables from a diskette into the computer and erase unused tables on the diskette.

The SAVE TBL command (number 62) is used to store a table on the diskette. When the SAVE TBL command is executed, that table is stored on the diskette under the specified name. When a table is saved, the specified name must begin with an alpanumeric character (A-Z) and have a total of 7 or fewer charcters.

The filename extension TBL is automatically added to the specified filename. Whenever a table is saved, the filename, title and dimensions of the table are entered in the file TABLE.DIR.

A file that was previously saved with a SAVE TBL command can be recovered again with the LOAD TBL command (number 61). To load a table into the computer, simply execute command number 61 (LOAD TBL) and enter the table name.

The ERASE TBL command (number 67) is used to eliminate a file that was saved on a diskette. When the ERASE TBL command is executed, the file TABLE. DIR is automatically updated. As a result, the file TABLE.DIR is a directory of the tables currently available on a diskette.

Command number 66 is the LIST TBLS command. When LIST TBLS is executed, a table directory will be listed on the printer. When command number 66 is executed, be sure that the printer is turned on and ready to operate.

## GENERAL INTEREST COMMANDS

### HELP

The HELP command (number 7) is used to display a brief explanation of a specified command. When command number 7 is executed, and the command number for which help is needed is then specified, a short description of the specified command appears at the bottom of the display.

### STOP

The STOP command (number 9) is used to return from the Profit Plan program to CP/M. When the STOP command is executed, the following prompt is displayed.

VERIFY (Y or N):*

If Y is used as a response to this prompt, a warm boot is performed, and the system prompt (A>) is displayed.

If N is the response to the prompt, the command has no effect, and the Profit Plan program is ready for another command.

### ROW RANGE

Command number 10 is the ROW RANGE command. This command is used to select the number of rows that are to be used in the table. Although more rows may appear on the display, only the specified range of rows are considered in calculations or in printed tables.

### COL RANGE

Command number 11 is the COL RANGE command. This command is used to select the number of columns that are to be used in the table. Although more columns may appear on the display, only the specified range of columns are considered in calculations or in printed tables.

## ORDER

The ORDER command, number 12, is used to select the order of calculations performed by the COMPUTE command. The ORDER command is used to cause the calculations to be performed exlusively along the columns or the rows of the worksheet. The ORDER command can also be used to cause the calculations to be performed along the columns and rows concurrently. The calculations can be performed on the rows before the columns, or vice versa. The importance of the order of operations is covered in a previous section of this chapter.

The first line of the display contains a message that describes the current order of operations. Since the default order of operations is rows before columns, the message appears as follows unless command number 12 is used to change the order.

ORDER=R/C

The four possible orders of operations are summarized in the following table.

**Table 7-6. Order of Operation Options**

| | |
|---|---|
| ORDER=R/O | Only the rows are calculated |
| ORDER=C/O | Only the columns are calculated |
| ORDER=R/C* | Rows are calculated before columns |
| ORDER=C/R | Columns are calculated before rows |

* Default mode

For example, if column number 3 is assigned the sum of the first two columns, this calculation will not be performed when the row only mode is in effect.

Similarly, if row number 3 is assigned the sum of the first two rows, this calculation will not be performed when the column only mode is in effect.

**SET DRIVE**

The SET DRIVE command (number 13) is used to select the disk drive where tables are recorded, stored and erased.

If drive B had been specified, be sure that drive B contains a diskette that has, or can receive the appropriate information. It is generally a good practice to use a blank, formatted diskette in drive B.

**SET UP**

Command number 14 is used to SET UP a table. It is convenient to use the SET UP command to select the number of rows and columns before the calculations begin. However, it is not always certain how many rows and columns are needed when a project begins.

Unfortunately, the SET UP command requires that all previous data on the table be erased. As a result, command number 14 can only be used at the beginning of a project.

**SET CRT**

Command number 15 is the SET CRT command. This command changes the original worksheet into a new format to be specified by the user. Three prompts will be displayed by SET CRT. These are outlined below:

The SET CRT command allows the user to select the number of decimal places (0 through 3) for each value on the display.

The SET CRT command is also used to specify the width of the row title area. This area can be assigned any width from 5 through 30 spaces.

The last parameter that can be chosen with the SET CRT command is the width of the data columns. These columns can be set from 4 through 20 columns wide.

**REORDER**

The REORDER command (number 28) is used to transpose two columns of the table. The REORDER command contains two prompts. The first prompt asks for the old column number, and the second prompt asks for the new column number. Actually, the "new" number and "old" number need not be distinguished. Effectively, the two specified columns are switched, no matter which is specified as "old" and which is specified as "new".

**GOTO**

The GOTO command (number 36) causes a specified section of the table to appear on the display. When more rows or columns are used in a table than can be displayed on the screen, it is impossible to view the entire table at one time. The GOTO command is used to "move" the table so that the specified rows and columns appear in the upper left-hand corner of the display.

**PLUG**

The PLUG command (number 37) is used to perform calculations with individual values within the table. The PLUG command enters the results of the calculations. Also, the PLUG command requires a formula in order to compute the value.

When the PLUG command is used, each value in the table will be represented by the letter V, followed by that value's row and column number separated with a comma. For example the formula:

V3,2 + V1,3

will cause the value in the third row of the second column to be added to the value in the first row of the third column. Keep in mind that multiplication and division are performed before addition and subtraction.

The PLUG command must be used carefully because the formula is stored as the formula to calculate an entire row of the table. When the COMPUTE command is executed the formula specified in the PLUG command will be used to calculate an entire row instead of a single value.

To avoid the problem of misusing the formula, enter the PLUG command only when the square brackets are located at a row that is not in use. Recall that the square brackets are used to indicate the row (or column) that the DATA commands affect.

## FIX

The FIX command (number 38) is used to calculate only one row or column of the table. The row or column that contains the square brackets will be recalculated when the FIX command is executed.

When the worksheet is used to perform calculations, each command is stored in the table so that the calculations can be repeated when the COMPUTE command is executed. The FIX command is used to perform one of these calculations for a single row or column. As a result, the FIX command cannot be used unless the row of the column had been assigned an appropriate calculation.

The FIX command is convenient to use when a table requires a special order of operations.

For example, if row number 3 is assigned the sum of the values in rows 1 and 2, and new data is inserted in row 1, the FIX command can be used to recalculate row 3 without recomputing the entire table. This can be achieved by moving the square brackets to the heading area of row 3 and executing command number 38. When this is done, the values in row 3 will be assigned the sums of the new values in row 1 and 2, but the other rows of the worksheet will not be affected.

**NULLIFY**

The NULLIFY command (number 39) is used to exclude one row or column from being calculated. When the NULLIFY command is executed, the data in the specified row or column will not be affected when a subsequent COMPUTE command is executed.

The NULLIFY command is generally used to prevent a set of data from being changed. When a section of the table has been prepared as desired, the NULLIFY command is used to preserve the data. After the NULLIFY command has been utilized, the COMPUTE command will have no effect on the row or column where the NULLIFY command was executed.

To NULLIFY a row or column, move the square brackets to the desired row or column heading and execute command number 39. In order to verify the action of the NULLIFY command, an additional (Y or N) response is required.

**CUMULATE**

The CUMULATE command (number 49) is used to calculate the sum of the values in a row (or column). The CUMULATE command is different from the SUM command, because CUMULATE generates an intermediate value for each number in the sum.

For example, consider a row of data with the values:

2 3 -2 4 6 -1 5

The sum of these values is 17. However, the results of the CUMULATIVE command for this data is as follows:

2 5 3 7 13 12 17

Notice that the second number in the result is the sum of the first two numbers in the original set of values. The third number in the result is the sum of the first three values in the original data, etc.

**GET**

The GET command (number 56) is used to copy an entire row or column of the table. The GET command simply makes a copy of a specified row or column in a different location.

The location of the new copy of data is specified by the location of the prompt (square brackets). The data that is to be copied must be specified in the GET command. If the square brackets enclose a column heading, the column to be copied must be specified. If the square brackets enclose a row heading, the row to be copied must be specified.

**FLOOR**

The FLOOR command (number 57) is used to establish a minimum value for a row or column. Any value that is less than the FLOOR value will be assigned the FLOOR value.

The FLOOR command can also be used to copy a row or column of data and impose a minimum value at the same time. The data will be copied from the specified row or column to the row or column that contains the square bracket prompt.

For example, if row one of the table has the values 1,2,3,4,5, and the prompt appears in row two, the FLOOR command can be used to make a modified copy of the data in row 1.

If a FLOOR value of 3 is specified for the data in row 1 while the prompt is in row 2, row number 2 will be assigned the values 3,3,3,4,5.

**CEILING**

The CEILING command (number 58) is used in a similar manner to the FLOOR command. However, the CEILING command imposes a maximum value on the data. The CEILING command requires that a row or column number be specified as well as a maximum value. The modified data will be assigned to the row or column that contains the prompt. Any data that exceeds the ceiling value will be assigned the ceiling value.

**CLR DATA**

The CLR DATA command is command number 63. This command erases all the values on the table, but nothing else. The row and column titles remain intact as well as the instructions for calculating the table.

**RESET**

The RESET command (number 64) erases all the information used with the Profit Plan program. The condition of the program after RESET has been executed is the same as when the program was started up.

**REDISPLAY**

The REDISPLAY command (number 65) is used to display the table in its standard format.

**REPORT**

The REPORT command (number 73) is used to generate printed copies of the table which appear on the display. The table is printed according to the specifications of the OPTIONS and TITLES commands.

## SAVE REP

The SAVE REP command is number 75. In order for a table to be started in a disk file, the SAVE REP command must be executed. SAVE REP causes the table to be stored in a disk file exactly as a printout of the table would appear.

The SAVE REP command, like the REPORT command, follows the specifications of the OPTIONS and TITLES commands.

A disk file titled OUTPUT.DIR is used as a directory of the output disk files. Each time command number 75 is used to save a table, the name, title and dimensions of the table are listed in the file OUTPUT.DIR.

# CHAPTER 8.
# WORD PLUS

## INTRODUCTION

The Word Plus software that is included with the Kaypro computer consists of several programs that are used to perform a wide variety of word processing functions.

Word Plus is generally used to determine the correct spelling of misspelled words. However, the package also includes programs that indicate the correct means of hyphenating words, as well as programs that prevent words from being misused.

### Getting Started

The Word Plus diskette that is provided with the Kaypro computer is very valuable. As a result, the master diskette should be promptly copied and stored in a safe place. In order to make a working copy of the master diskette, use the FORMAT, COPY and SYSGEN commands as described in Chapter 2.

Since the Word Plus programs are generally used with files that are created with Perfect Writer, be sure to create the document files on the diskette in drive B. This allows the proper programs and document files to be accessed with a minimal amount of diskette swapping. However, when a file is stored on the diskette in drive B, the drive specifier (B:) must be included in the filename.

## CORRECTING THE SPELLING ERRORS IN A FILE

Suppose the following file was created with the Perfect Writer.

> A compter consists of hardwere and softwere. The hardware refers to the system's phisical devices, and the software refers to the instrucsions that maie the hardware perform useful tusks.

This document obviously has many spelling errors. One of the Word Plus programs, TW, can be used to correct the spelling errors in this file.

Notice the word "tusks" at the end of the document file. Even though this word is a mistake, the TW program will not be able to find this error. The word "tusks" is used in the file instead of "tasks", but "tusks" is a valid word, and correctly spelled. Although the spelling checker can locate spelling errors, it cannot locate an instance where an incorrect word was used in a document.

To begin using the TW program, insert a working copy of the Word Plus diskette in drive A, and the diskette containing the document file in drive B. Press the Reset switch to initialize the system.

The following message should appear on the display.

```
KAYPRO II
64k CP/M v 2.2

A>
```

If this message does not appear on the monitor, the Word Plus diskette probably does not contain a copy of the operating system. If this problem occurs, perform the SYSGEN procedure described in Chapter 2 with the Word Plus diskette.

When the system prompt (A>) is displayed, type the program name TW and press the Return key. The disk drive will begin operating and the following message will be displayed:

```
—The WORD Plus—   Version 1.22
 Copyright 1981 - Oasis Systems

 Name of file to check?:
```

In response to this prompt, enter the document filename and be sure to include the drive specifier. The example presented here will have the filename B:TEXT.MMS.

When the filename is specified, a list of options will be displayed on the monitor. These options need only be specified the first time that the TW program is used. The selections are used to set up the Word Plus program to work with a particular word processor.

```
Special dictionary name?:
Save context info? Y/N (Ret=N)   :Y
Ignore lines starting with? (Type char, Ret=No)   :
Ignore UPPER case words? Y/N (Ret=N)   :
Ignore text between? (Type char, Ret=None)   :
Mark words that change length? Y/N (Ret=N)   :
Marking character   :*
Save new defaults? Y/N (Ret=N)   :Y
```

To begin using the Word Plus program, simply press the Return key in response to all the options except the second and the last. These two options require the Y response.

The program proceeds by displaying the following summary:

```
          — Summary —

Checking file   :   B:TEXT.MMS
Saving context info
Marking character  → *

These are the current settings
Press return to proceed, or space to change
```

This list is a review of the options that are currently in effect. Press the space bar if you wish to change any of these options. When the space bar is pressed, the prompts are once again displayed. The last prompt displayed (Save new defaults) is used to indicate that a permanent copy of the preceding selections should be stored for future use. When a Y response is used with this last prompt, the options will not be displayed in any subsequent TW program calls. When the "save defaults" options is in effect, the program skips directly from the "Special dictionary name?" prompt to the summary of the current options.

To proceed with the program, press the Return key. The following message will be displayed while the spelling of the file is checked. This procedure may require several seconds or even a few minutes to complete.

```
SPELL+ Version 1.4
Copyright 1981 - Oasis Systems

Compiling Word List
20 Unique Words
Checking Main Dictionary
```

When the program has completed checking the file, the following message will be displayed:

```
Checking Update Dictionary
Writing File to Disk
6 unmatched words.
```

The program proceeds by allowing the user to correct the spelling errors that appear in the file. The program arranges the misspelled words in alphabetical order and displays each word individually. The following display will be presented when the first correction is ready to be made.

```
REVIEW+ Version 1.2, Copyright 1981 - Oasis Systems

Add word to:                              Other options:
   U > pdate Dictionary                      P > revious word
   S >pec. Dict. "SPECIALS.CMP"              N>  ext word
M > ark word                                 R > esume review
D >iscard word                               L >ook up word
C >orrect word                               V>  iew context

 →COMPTER -
```

The display includes the copyright message, the list of commands, and the first word of the file to be corrected. Each time a misspelled word is displayed at the bottom of the screen, a letter that corresponds to one of the commands must be entered. The use of each command is described in Table 8-1.

**Table 8-1. Spelling Correction Commands**

| | |
|---|---|
| U | Add the word to the Update Dictionary. This dictionary will be automatically checked each time the program is executed. |
| S | Add the word to the Special Dictionary. This file is used to store unrecognized words for future reference. |
| M | Mark the word with the specified mark character, but do not make any corrections in the file. |
| D | Leave the word unchanged and proceed with the next unrecognized word. |
| C | Make the following correction. The correct spelling of the word must follow. |
| L | Look up the word and present a selection of correctly spelled words. |
| V | Display the line of the file in which the misspelled word appears. |
| P | Return to the preceding misspelled word. |
| N | Proceed to the next misspelled word. |
| R | Resume the review of misspelled words. |

If the "misspelled" word is in fact correctly spelled even though the program could not recognize it, select the D (Discard Word) or U (Update Dictionary) command. If the word is only used once in a while, the "Discard word" selection is probably the best choice. However, if the word is commonly used, it can be added to the update dictionary. This selection allows the word to be recognized when it is used in the future.

If you would like to compile a new dictionary, the "Special Dictionary" command can be used. This command causes the unrecognized word to be saved in the file "SPECIAL. CMP" (unless a filename was specified in response to the "Special dictionary name?" prompt). The words that are saved in this file are not added to the dictionary. They are only saved for future reference.

The "Mark word" selection is used to insert a special character before an unrecognized word. This allows the file to be easily corrected with the Perfect Writer program. The character that is inserted before an unmatched word can be specified in the original questionaire provided by the program. If no special character was specified, an asterisk (*) will be used by the Mark word command.

The "Discard word" selection is used to ingore an unmatched word in a file. The word remains unchanged and it is not added to the update dictionary or the special dictionary.

If an unrecognized word needs to be corrected, there are two commands that can be used to assist in correcting the word. These two commands are "Look up word" and "View context".

The "Look up word" command is used to provide a list of possible words that can be used to replace the unrecognized word. For example, if the "maie" is included in a file, the TW program will not recognize the word. If the "Look up word" selection is chosen from the menu, a list of possible replacement words is displayed as follows.

```
0 mace    5 mail     ! make     * marie
1 made    6 maim     # male     + mate
2 mae     7 main     $ mamie    / maze
3 maia    8 maine    % mane
4 maid    9 maize    & mare
```

After the list of correctly spelled words has been displayed, the menu will again appear on the display. In order to change the unmatched word to one of the words in the list, choose selection C from the menu.

When the C selection is chosen, the prompt at the bottom of the display appears as follows:

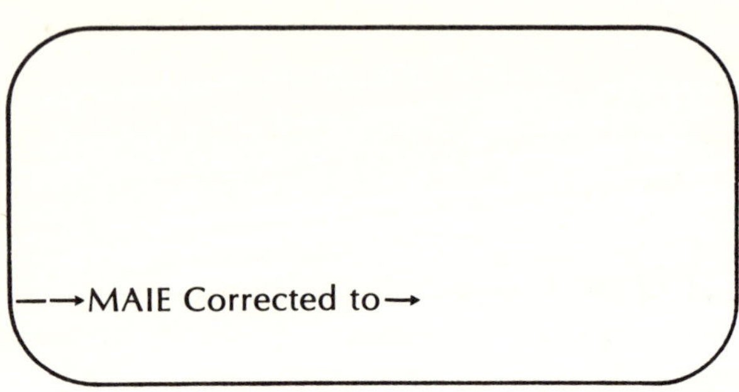


If you would like to change the word "maie" into one of the words in the list, simply type the number or character that corresponds to the desired word on the list and press Return. In the case of our example, enter an exclamation mark (!) in order to change "maie" to "make".

If you know the correct spelling of a word that is misspelled, you can correct the word without using the "Look up word" command. To correct a word in this fashion, simply type "C" to correct the word, and enter the correct spelling of the word. This method is much faster to use than the "Look up word" command.

If you are not sure of the word that you wish to use in a document, you can use the "View context" command to display the line of the document that contains the unrecognized word.

For example, if the "View context" command was chosen for the word "maie" in the file B:TEXT.MMS, the following display will appear:

```
ers to the instrucsions that maie the hardware perform useful

REVIEW+ Version 1.2, Copyright 1981 - Oasis Systems

Add word to:                               Other options:
  U>pdate Dictionary                         P>revious word
  S>pec. Dict. "SPECIALS.CMP"                N>ext word
M>ark word                                   R>esume review
D>iscard word                                L>ook up word
C>orrect word                                V>iew context

– →MAIE -
```

When the menu reappears, any of the commands can be used in the same way as before. All of the commands will have the same function before and after the "View context" command has been executed.

When the TW program has been used to review some of the unrecognized words in a file, the "Previous word" command can be used to return to a word that was already reviewed. The "Previous word" command is convenient to use when you would like to change the selection you chose for a preceding word.

The words in the file are not changed until the review of unrecognized words is complete. As a result, you can always change your selections until you press the Return key at the end of the review of the list of words.

Just as you use the "Previous word" command to observe the selection for a preceding unrecognized word, you can also use the "Next word" command to proceed forward through the list. The "Resume review" command is used to return to the word that was being reviewed before any "Previous word" commands were executed.

The "Next word" and "Resume review" commands do not have any effect until a "Previous word" command is executed.

The review session is complete when each unrecognized word in a file has been either ignored, changed or added to a dictionary. When the review is complete, the following message will appear at the bottom of the display:

```
End of list. Press "return" if done.
```

When the preceding prompt appears on the display, use the "Previous word" command if you would like to review one of your selections. If you would like to proceed by making the corrections in the file, simply press the Return key.

When the Return key was used in response to the "End of list" prompt, the following message will appear on the display:

```
MARKFIX+ Version 1.4
Copyright 1981 - Oasis Systems
```

This section of the program is used to make the corrections in the file. Before the contents of your document file are altered in any way, the original file will be copied and placed in a "backup" file.

A backup file will be created with the same filename as the original file, except for the filename extension. Backup files are assigned the filename extension .BAK. For example, the file B:TEXT.BAK would be generated by the computer before the contents of B:TEXT.MMS would be altered.

When the TW program has been completed, a message will be displayed that summarizes the results of the program. The following display is a typical summary of the TW program results.

```
2 words marked
3 words corrected
3 words changed length. *reform*
```

After this summarization has been displayed, the following message will appear on the display.

```
Completed file B:TEXT.MMS
Warm Boot

A>
```

The system prompt (A>) will be displayed when the program has been completed. This indicates that the computer is ready to begin another program.

## Spell

The Spell program can be used to output a list of the words in a document that are not found in the standard dictionary. The Spell program can list the unrecognized words on the display or the printer. The output can also be stored in a disk file.

The Spell program can only be called when the system prompt (A>) appears. The format of the Spell program consists of the Spell program name, the document filename and the optional output device specifiers.

The simplest application of the program is to list the unrecognized words on the display. Consider a document in the disk file B:TEXT.MMS. The following statement causes the output to appear on the monitor:

```
A>SPELL B:TEXT.MMS
```

The output can be sent to the system printer by adding the characters "$P" at the end of the statement. The following example causes the output to occur at the printer.

```
A>SPELL B:TEXT.MMS $P
```

If the output device specifier "$PL" is used, the list of unmatched words is sent to the display as well as the printer.

When "$FA" or "$FB" are used as the output device specifier, the list of unrecognized words is sent to the disk file ERRWORDS.TXT. The last letter in the device specifier (A or B) indicates the disk drive in which the file is created. For example, the specifier "$FB" causes the output to be sent to the file B:ERRWORDS.TXT.

The output can be sent to any combination of the three output devices simultaneously. For example, the following statement causes the output to appear on the display while the unrecognized words are also output to the file B:ERRWORDS.TXT.

A>SPELL B:TEXT.MMS $LFB

**Homonyms**

Homonyms are words that are easily confused because they are pronounced the same, even though they are spelled differently. These words are commonly confused, but a spelling checker cannot locate these problems.

The Word Plus diskette contains a file with more than 800 homonyms. This file can be used with the Markfix program to locate possible problem areas in a document.

You are probably familiar with most of the commonly used words in the file HOMONYMS.TXT. Some examples of commonly used homonyms are as follows.

to too two
sail sale
throne thrown

As a result, it is generally a good idea to make another copy of the file HOMONYMS.TXT, and use Perfect Writer to delete those homonyms with which you are familiar. This new revised homonyms file allows the program to be executed more quickly. Also, using the new file avoids the annoying problem of being notified each time you use a simple homonym.

If you choose to edit the homonym file, as recommended previously, be sure to use the PIP command to make a backup copy of the original file before you begin editing (see Chapter 2).

The Markfix command can be used to search a document and place a special character before each word that occurs in another file. For example, if the Markfix program is used to check a document file against the homonym file, an asterisk (*) is used to mark all the homonyms that appear in the document file.

Consider the file B:FOOD.MMS that contains the following sentence.

I went two the store too by wry bred.

Although each word in this file is spelled correctly, there are 5 misused homonyms.

In order to check this file for possible problems, execute the following command:

A>MARKFIX B:FOOD.MMS HOMONYMS.TXT ↵

When the Markfix procedure is complete the B:FOOD.MMS file will appear as follows.

I went *two the store *too *by *wry *bred.

Each homonym in the file is preceded by an asterisk to warn the user that the words are easily confused. The original document is stored in the file B:FOOD.BAK. If you wish to make any corrections to the file, use the Perfect Writer text editor.

### Markfix

The Markfix program can also be used to replace a word throughout a file. For example, if you have a document that describes a machine, but the machine has been replaced by a new model, you can revise the entire document with the Markfix program.

For example, the document B:MANUAL.MMS may contain the following text:

> This manual provides the operating instructions
> for the Wondertoast toaster...

If the new model of the toaster is called Fantistictoast, the same manual can be used if the name of the toaster is the only information that has been changed.

In order to use the Markfix program to change the words in a file, it is necessary to create a file that contains the corrections. The format of a correction file is as follows:

*oldword1/newword1*
*oldword2/newword2*
*etc.*

The slash (/) is used to separate the word that is to be replaced from the new word that is to be inserted in its place. For example, in order to replace "Wondertoast" with "Fantastictoast", create the file B:NEWMODEL.MMS with the following contents.

Wondertoast/Fantastictoast

Statements similar to the "toast" example can be included for as many corrections as are necessary. Each pair of words should be placed on a separate line of the correction file.

The format used in making these corrections in the original document file is as follows.

A>MARKFIX B:MANUAL.MMS B:NEWMODEL.MMS

When the Markfix procedure has been completed, the contents of the file B:MANUAL.MMS will be as follows.

> This manual provides the operating instructions for the Fantastictoast toaster...

The original contents of the file will be stored in the file B:MANUAL.BAK.

**Lookup**

The Lookup program is used to find a list of correctly spelled words that are similar to the specified word. Like the other Word Plus programs, the Lookup program can only be called when the system prompt is displayed.

The Lookup program cannot locate the correct spelling of a word unless you have a general idea of how the word is actually spelled. As a result, the Lookup program name must be followed by your best guess of the correct spelling of a word.

For example, execute the following statement.

A>LOOKUP DICTIONAIRY

The computer responds with the following message:

```
LOOKUP - VER 2.0,
Copyright 1981 - Oasis Systems
```

The program searches for correctly spelled words that are spelled in a manner similar to the specified word. In this example, the only word that can be found is DICTIONARY. If many words are similar to the specified word, each possibility will be displayed.

If the Lookup program locates a word that is spelled exactly like the specified word, an asterisk (*) will be displayed to the right of the output. If the program cannot locate any words that are similar to the specified word, the program ends without generating any output.

The Lookup program generally searches for words that have the same first letter as the specified word. If you are not sure of the first letter of the specified word, you can conduct a "long search" by adding the characters "$L" to the end of the Lookup statement. Since the entire dictionary must be searched when the first character is unknown, a "long search" takes much longer than a normal search.

For example, the following statement requires more than a minute to locate the word "occult".

LOOKUP ACCULT $L

**WC**

The WC program is used to count the number of words in a file. To execute the WC program, include the name of the program, followed by the filename.

The results of the WC program for a typical file are as follows.

```
A>WC B:FILE.MMS
WORD COUNT+ Version 1.1
Copyright 1981 - Oasis Systems
There are 610 words in the file.
```

## Wordfreq

The Wordfreq program is used to determine the number of times each word appears in a file. This program is generally used to indicate the words in a document that are overused or repetitious.

The Wordfreq program can be used to generate the list of words used in the document in alphabetical order, or in order according to the number of times the word was used. Normally, the output will be generated in order of usage. However, the characters "$A" can be used at the end of the Wordfreq statement to generate a list in alphabetical order.

When a Wordfreq statement is executed, a message will appear on the display in the following format.

```
2,591   Total words
508     Unique words
234     Words appearing once
```

This message displays the total number of words in the document, the number of different words and the number of words that appear only once in the document.

The actual list of words, and the number of times each word appears in the document, do not appear on the display. The output is sent to a disk file that has the same filename as the original document, but a different filename extension. Output files from the Wordfreq program always have the filename extension .FRQ.

For example, the document file B:TEXT.MMS would have a Wordfreq output file with the name B:TEXT.FRQ. The following statement would cause the Wordfreq program to compile a list of words appearing in the file B:TEXT.MMS.

```
A>WORDFREQ B:TEXT.MMS
```

This example causes the output file B:TEXT.FRQ to include the following entries:

```
231   THE
94    TO
76    YOU
58    A
48    WE
     etc.
```

The word list can also be generated in alphabetical order by adding the characters "$A"at the end of the statement.

```
A>WORDFREQ B:TEXT.MMS $A
```

This format of the Wordfreq statement causes the output file B:TEXT.FRQ to include the following entries:

```
58   A
1    ABANDON
4    ABOUT
1    ABOVE
2    ADD
         etc.
```

**Find**

The Find program is used primarily for solving crossword puzzles and similar games. The program is used to find words that contain an unknown character or group of characters.

The question mark (?) is used to represent an unknown character and an asterisk (*) is used to represent an unknown group of characters. These two characters are used along with a known character or a group of characters.

For example, the Find program can be used to determine a set of five letter words that begin with "S" and end with "R". The following example demonstrates the correct format for this Find statement.

A>FIND S???R

The program returns 35 words that have five letters, begin with "S" and end with "R".

To obtain a list of words that begin with "S" and end with "ABLE", execute the following command:

A>FIND S*ABLE

This statement causes a list of 21 words that fit this description to be displayed on the monitor.

Although many question marks can be used with each Find program, only one asterisk can appear in each entry.

**Anagram**

The Anagram program is used to "unscramble" a set of characters and return a set of correctly spelled words that consist of the specified characters. For example, the letters A, E, D, and R can be used to spell the words dear, read, and dare.

The Anagram program uses the following format.

A>ANAGRAM AEDR

This example causes the words DARE, DEAR and READ to be returned.

The question mark (?) can be used with the Anagram program to represent any character. For example, if you wish to determine a list of four letter words that contain the letter Z, execute the following command.

```
A>ANAGRAM ???Z
```

### Hyphen

The Hyphen program provided with Word Plus is used to determine the locations in which a word can be hyphenated.

Many word processors allow special characters to be inserted in a file to indicate where long words may be hyphenated. Unfortunately, the Perfect Writer does not recognize any special characters for this purpose. As a result, the utility of the Hyphen program is strictly limited by Perfect Writer.

Because of the complexities and exceptions in the English language, the Hyphen program returns incorrect hyphenations quite regularly. As a result, the Hyphen program must be used carefully.

When the Hyphen program is executed, a question mark (?) will indicate that the program is ready to accept a word. Respond by typing the word that you would like to hyphenate. When the word has been entered, press the Return key.

The word will be returned with dashes inserted between the syllables of the word. The question mark prompt will appear after each word has been returned.

To exit the Hyphen program, press Control-C. The following sequence demonstrates the correct format of the Hyphen program.

```
A>HYPHEN
HYPHEN+ Version 2.2
Copyright 1982 - Oasis Systems

Reading HYEXCEPT.TXT file

?INCONSPICUOUS
IN-CON-SPICUOUS

?↑C
Warm Boot
```

The Hyphen program uses a file of exceptions to make the program more reliable. Unfortunately, the procedure for modifying the exception file is rather involved. If you need an accurate hyphenation program, consult the Word Plus documentation supplied with the master diskette.

**Dictsort**

The Dictsort program can be used to alphabetize the words in a file. This program creates a backup file of the original file, with the same filename, except for the filename extension. The filename extension of the backup file is .BAK.

The Dictsort program does not repeat any of the words in the final output. As a result, any repetitive words in the original file will only be listed once in the alphabetized file. Also, each word in the output file is placed on a separate line.

**Adding New Entries to the Dictionary**

If you use a large number of words that are not included in the dictionary, you can use the Perfect Writer program to add these words to the update dictionary. The update dictionary will be checked each time the TW program is executed. As a result, words that are added to the update dictionary will be considered valid words.

The update dictionary is stored in the disk file UPDICT.CMP. Initially, this file contains the commands that are used with Perfect Writer. Words like FLUSHLEFT and BLANKSPACE are included in the update dictionary to prevent problems when the Perfect Writer commands are used in a file.

To add words to the file UPDICT.CMP, insert the Perfect Writer diskette in drive A, and the Word Plus diskette in drive B. Press the Reset switch and enter the MENU command in response to the system prompt. Choose selection E from the menu, and specify B:UPDICT.CMP as the file to be edited.

Type the words in the file that you would like to add to the dictionary. When all the new words have been added to the file, be sure to save the new version of the file. Recall that the Control-X, Control-S command is used to save a file. Control-X, Control-C is the command that is used to return to the Perfect Writer menu.

When the file has been saved, remove the Perfect Writer diskette, and insert the Word Plus diskette in drive A. Be sure to use the Control-C command to perform a warm boot after swapping diskettes.

The TW program cannot use the update dictionary unless the words are in alphabetical order. As a result, whenever the file UPDICT.CMP is modified, be sure to execute the following command.

A>DICTSORT UPDICT.CMP

This step completes the modification of the dictionary.

# CHAPTER 9.
# PROGRAMMING IN MICROSOFT BASIC

## INTRODUCTION

The Kaypro computer includes the Microsoft programming language in the standard software package. A programming language is a tool that is used to write programs with a set of instructions that are easy to understand. Many of the commands used in Microsoft BASIC are words that are commonly used in everyday spoken and written English (i.e. CALL, LOAD, WHILE, etc.).

Microsoft BASIC is a commonly used language because of its versatility and simplicity. These qualities make Microsoft BASIC an excellent language for writing applications programs.

### Getting Started

The Microsoft BASIC diskette that is provided with the Kaypro computer is very valuable. In order to prevent the information on the diskette from being accidentally erased, make a working copy of the master diskette and store the master diskette in a safe place. Be sure to use a blank, formatted diskette to make a working copy. Also, be sure to include a copy of the operating system on the working diskette.

The procedure for preparing a diskette with the FORMAT, COPY and SYSGEN commands is outlined in detail in Chapter 2. Be sure to format an additional diskette in order to store miscellaneous programs and data.

When the Kaypro is powered on, the following message appears on the display.

```
*KAYPRO II*

Please insert your diskette into Drive A
```

When the working copy of the Microsoft BASIC diskette is inserted in drive A, the following message should appear on the display shortly after the drive door is closed.

```
KAYPRO II
64k CP/M v 2.2

A>
```

In response to the system prompt (A>), type the following command.

A><u>MBASIC</u>

After the disk drive operates for several seconds the following message is displayed.

```
BASIC-80 Rev. 5.21
[CP/M Version]
Copyright 1977-1981 (c) by Microsoft
Created: 28-Jul-81
34872 Bytes free
Ok
```

"Ok" is the BASIC prompt that notifies the user that the computer is ready for a BASIC command.

**Creating and Editing Programs**

Only one program can be present in the computer's memory at any time. Also, the program that is in the computer's memory is erased when the computer is shut off. As a result, it is necessary to store program files on a diskette.

Program lines can be added to a program in the computer's memory simply by typing them on the keyboard. For example, type the following lines when the BASIC prompt is displayed.

```
Ok
10 FOR T=1 TO 10
20 PRINT T*T;
30 NEXT T
```

If an error is made while the program line is being entered, simply use the BACKSPACE key to eliminate the error. Then, enter the correct line.

Once a line has been entered into the program, the EDIT feature must be used to change the line. In order to change the program line, enter the word EDIT, followed by the line number of the statement that needs to be corrected. When the EDIT command is entered, the line number is returned in the following line, followed by the cursor.

**Example**

```
EDIT 20
20
```

The space bar is used to move the cursor through the program line. When the cursor is moved to the right, the portion of the program line that is to the left of the cursor is displayed.

In the EDIT mode, the D key is used to delete characters that are to the right of the cursor. When the D key is used, the deleted character is displayed between two backslashes.

**Example**

```
EDIT 20
20 PRINT T*T\;\
```

In the preceding example, the cursor is moved through the program statement by pressing the space bar. When the cursor has been located after the last T in the statement, the D key is pressed. Since the semicolon is one space to the right of the T, the semicolon is deleted. The backslashes indicate that the semicolon has been deleted.

The I key is used to insert characters into the program line. In the edit mode, when the I key is pressed, any subsequent typed characters will be inserted into the statement. In order to exit from the insert mode, press the ESC key.

Illustration 9-1 contains an example of the usage of the Microsoft BASIC editor.

If a serious error is made when a line is entered, it may be desireable to "start from scratch". A new line can be entered in place of the old line simply by typing the line number of the incorrect line and entering the correct line.

For example, if line 10 in a program is incorrect, simply enter line 10 again with the correct statements. The new line 10 takes the place of the old line 10.

Illustration 9-2. contains an example of editing a program by replacing a line.

**Illustration 9-1. Using the Microsoft BASIC Editor**

| | |
|---|---|
| 40 FOR T 10 TO 20 | Enter line 40 |
| EDIT 40 | Enter the EDIT mode |
| 40 | Computer responds |
| 40 FOR | Press the space bar four times |
| 40 FOR \T\ | Press D to delete the T |
| 40 FOR\T\ | Press the I key to insert |
| 40 FOR\T\R | Press the R key |
| 40 FOR\T\R | Press the ESC key to stop inserting |
| 40 FOR\T\R = 10 TO | Press the space bar 9 times |
| 40 FOR\T\R = 10 TO \2\ | Press D to delete the 2 |
| 40 FOR\T\R = 10 TO \2\ | Press the I key to insert |
| 40 FOR\T\R=10 TO\2\3 | Press the 3 key |
| 40 FOR\T\R=10 TO\2\30 | Press Return to stop editing |
| LIST 40 | Enter LIST command |
| 40 FOR R = 10 TO 30 | Review the Results |

**Illustration 9-2. Editing a Program by Replacement**

| | |
|---|---|
| 10 FOR J=1 TO 100 | Enter line 10 |
| 20 PRINT J | Enter line 20 |
| 30 NEXT J | Enter line 30 |
| 10 FOR J=1 TO 200 | Enter the new line 10 |
| LIST | List the program |
| 10 FOR J=1 TO 200 | Review the results of the edit |
| 20 PRINT J | |
| 30 NEXT J | |

A line can be deleted from a program simply by entering the line number, followed by Return. For example, to delete line 10 from a program, simply enter 10 followed by Return. This is equivalent to replacing line 10 with a line that does not contain a statement.

The Perfect Writer program can be used to edit Microsoft BASIC programs, but the procedure generally requires a great deal of disk swapping. If a great deal of editing needs to be done, the Perfect Writer may be more convenient. However, troubleshooting a program will be very difficult unless the Microsoft BASIC Editor has been mastered.

## Saving and Loading Program Files

When you would like to save a program that you have written, use the SAVE command to store the program in a disk file. For example, to store a basic program called GRADES on the diskette in drive B, execute the following BASIC command.

```
SAVE "B:GRADES.BAS"
```

It is recommended that all Microsoft BASIC programs be stored on a diskette in drive B with the filename extension .BAS.

Once a program file is saved, it can be recovered with a LOAD statement. This statement can only be used in Microsoft BASIC. A LOAD statement has no effect if it is executed when the system prompt (A>) is displayed. The following statement is an example of the correct format of a LOAD statement.

```
LOAD "B:GRADES.BAS"
```

**Games**

There are several games that are included with the standard software package of the Kaypro computer. These games are all included on the Microsoft BASIC diskette. Each game is stored in a disk file with the filename extension of .BAS or .COM. The following list contains the names of the game program files.

CATCHUM.COM
LADDER.COM
ALIENS.COM
STRTRK.BAS
CHASE.BAS
TRADE.BAS
HORSE.BAS
BLKJK.BAS
WUMP.BAS
ROCKET.BAS
TAXMAN.BAS
BIO.BAS

The three files that have the filename extension .COM can be executed directly from CP/M. When the system prompt appears, simply enter the program name and press the Return key to begin the game. The remaining nine programs can only be used in Microsoft BASIC. As a result, these games require a LOAD statement as described above (without the drive specifier B:) as well as the RUN command to begin the program.

## Microsoft BASIC Command Summary

In this section, we will present brief descriptions of the various commands, statements, and functions used in Microsoft BASIC. If you wish a more complete description of the various Microsoft BASIC commands as well as a tutorial on Microsoft BASIC programming, please refer to the IBM PC & XT User's Handbook. The IBM PC also uses Microsoft BASIC.

The following rules and abbreviations will be followed in this chapter in our configuration descriptions of the various Microsoft BASIC commands, statements, and functions.

1. Any capitalized words are keywords. These may be input in either uppercase, lowercase, or both. BASIC automatically converts keywords to uppercase.

2. Any words, phrases, or letters shown in lowercase italics identify an entry that must be made by the operator.

3. Any items enclosed in brackets [ ] are optional.

4. An ellipsis (...) shows that an item may be repeated as often as desired.

5. Any punctuation marks, except the square brackets, (ex. ; , =) must be included where they are shown.

### Commands, Statements, and Functions

**ABS** *(argument)*

Returns the absolute value of the *argument*.

**ASC** *(argument)*

Returns the ASCII code for first character of a string *argument*.

**ATN** *(argument)*

Returns the arctangent of the *argument* in radians.

**AUTO** *(line [,increment])*

Automatic generation of line numbers. The beginning line number is specified in *line*. The increment to be used in generating new line numbers is specified in *increment*. The default for both *line* and *increment* is 10.

If the *line* is followed by a comma but not by an *increment* value, the last *increment* specified in an AUTO command is used.

If AUTO generates a line number which is already in use, an asterisk will be displayed following the new line number being generated. This serves as a warning to the user that any entries for this line will replace the existing line in memory. If the user responds to the new line number by pressing Return immediately following the asterisk, the original line in memory will be saved, and a subsequent new line number will be generated. Press Control-C to cancel AUTO.

**CALL** *address (argument, argument...)*

Used to call a machine language program.

**CBDL** *(argument)*

Converts its *argument* to a double precision number.

**CHAIN** [MERGE] *filespec* [,[*line*] [,ALL] [,DELETE *line-line*]

Transfers control to another program given in *filespec* and passes variables to is from the current program.

If the option *line* is specified, execution will begin at that point.

If the ALL option is specified, every variable in the current program will be passed to the program being called. If ALL is not specified, the current program must contain a common statement which will indicate the variables to be passed to the program being called.

If the MERGE option is included, a section of the code may be brought into the BASIC program as an overlay. In other words, a MERGE operation will be performed with the current program and the program being CHAIN'ed. The program being CHAIN'ed must be an ASCII file if it is to be MERGE'd.

An example of the use of the MERGE command in a CHAIN statement is given below;

```
CHAIN MERGE "A:NEW", 100
```

In this example, the program NEW on drive A will be brought into the program as an overlay with a starting point for execution in line 100.

Once an overlay has been used, it is generally deleted so that a new overlay can be instituted. This is accomplished with the DELETE option. The DELETE option, when used in the CHAIN statement, functions much like the DELETE command.

In the following example,

```
CHAIN MERGE "A:NEW", 1000, DELETE 1000-3000
```

lines 1000 through 3000 in the current program will be deleted before the loading of the overlay.

**CHR$** *(argument)*

Converts an ASCII code to its corresponding character.

**CINT** *(argument)*

Converts its *argument* to an integer by rounding.

**CLEAR** [,[,*byte1*] [,*byte2*]]

Sets all numeric variables to zero and string variables to null. Optionally used to set the end of memory and the amount of stack space.

**CLOAD** *filename*

CLOAD is used to load a program from cassette tape into RAM.

**CLOSE** [#] *filenumber,...*

Closes file(s) indicated.

**COMMON** *variables*

Used to pass *variables* to program being chained.

**CONT**

Used to continue program execution after a Control-C, STOP, or END was used to stop execution.

**COS** *(argument)*

Returns the cosine of its argument in radians.

**CSAVE** *(filename)*

Used to save the program currently stored in RAM on cassette tape.

**CSNG** *(argument)*

Converts its argument to a single precision number.

**CVD** *(argument)*

Converts its argument (an 8 byte string) to a numeric value.

**CVI** *(argument)*

Converts its argument (a 2 byte string) to a numeric value.

**CVS** *(argument)*

Converts its argument (a 4 byte string) to a numeric value.

**DATA** *constant,...*

Contains numeric and string constants later accessed by READ statements.

**DEF FN** *function name* (variable,...) = *function*

Used to define a string or numeric function.

**DEFDBL** *(variable...)*

Declares variable type as double precision.

**DEFINT** *variable...*

Declares variable type as integer.

**DEFSNG** *variable...*

Declares variable type as single precision numeric.

**DEFSTR** *variable...*

Declares variable type as string.

**DEF USR** [N] = *address*

Defines the starting address for a machine language subroutine named in N.

**DELETE** [*line1*] [– *line2*]

Used to delete program lines. If only *line 1* is specified, only that line will be deleted. If only *line 2* is specified with a dash, all lines from the beginning of the program through *line 2* will be deleted. If both *line 1* and *line 2* are specified, all lines within that range will be deleted.

**DIM** *variable (subscript,...)*

Used to declare array variables. If an array variable is used without a DIM statement, that variable is automatically dimensioned for 10 elements.

**EDIT** *line*

Used to display a line for editing purposes.

**END**

Used to stop the program. Closes files and returns to command level.

**EOF** *(filenumber)*

Used to test for end of file condition. A –1 is returned if the end of a sequential file has been reached.

**ERASE** *variable*

Used to erase arrays from a program after they have been dimensioned.

**ERL**

Returns error line number.

**ERR**

Returns error code.

**ERROR** *N*

Allows user to simulate the error code given, or to define his own error code.

**EXP** *(argument)*

Raises e to the power given in *argument*.

**FIELD** *filenumber, N* **AS** *variable*

Defines a field in a random file buffer.

**FIX** *(argument)*

Truncates *argument* to an integer.

**FOR** *variable =argument 1* **TO** *argument 2* [**STEP** *argument*]
**NEXT** *variable*

Executes a sequence of statements a specified number of times.

**FRE** (*argument*)

The argument for FRE is a dummy argument. FRE returns the free bytes in memory.

**GET** [#] *filenumber* [*,record number*]

Used to read a record from a random access disk file into a random buffer.

**GOSUB** *line*

Branches a subroutine at the specified *line*.

**GOTO** *line*

Branches to the line specified.

**HEX$** *(argument)*

Converts *argument* to a hexadecimal string.

**IF** *expression* **THEN** *statement:...*[**ELSE** *statement:...*]

Executes the *statement(s)* following THEN when *expression* evaluates as true. Otherwise *statement* following ELSE or next program statement is executed.

**INKEY$**

Reads a character from the keyboard.

**INP**

Reads a byte from the port specified.

**INPUT** [[;] *prompt* {; ,}] *variable...*

Used to assign data from the keyboard to variables.

**INPUT#** *filenumber, variable...*

Used to read data from the specified file and assign that value to the variable named.

**INPUT$** *(N, filenumber)*

Used to read N characters from the specified file.

**INSTR** ([*N*,] *x$, y$*)

Returns the position where one string (*y$*) appears within another string (*x$*). *N* indicates the starting character position within *x$* where the search is to begin.

**INT** *(argument)*

Returns the largest integer less than or equal to its argument.

**KILL** *"filespec"*

Used to erase a diskette file.

**LEFT$** *(N, string)*

Returns the leftmost N characters in the string specified.

**LEN** (*x$*)

Returns the number of characters in the string indicated.

**LET** *variable = expression*

Assigns the value in *expression* to *variable*.

**LINE INPUT** *prompt; variable$*

Used to read an entire line from the keyboard, and assign that data to the specified variable.

**LINE INPUT#** *filenumber, variable$*

Used to read an entire line from a file, and assign that data to the specified variable.

**LIST** [*n-m*]

Used to list program lines specified on the screen. When list is executed without any parameter, the entire program will be displayed.

**LLIST** [*n-m*]

Used to list lines specified to the printer.

**LOAD** *"filespec"*

Used to load a program file from disk into RAM.

**LOC** *(filenumber)*

Returns the record number position within the specified random access file.

**LOG** *(argument)*

Returns the natural logarithm of its *argument*.

**LPOS** *(argument)*

Returns the position of the print head. The argument has no effect on the value returned.

**LPRINT** [*data*]
**LPRINT USING** [*data*]

Sends data to the printer. (See PRINT and PRINT USING)

**LSET** *variable$ = string*

Left justifies a string in the random file buffer.

**MERGE** *"filespec"*

Used to merge the specified program with the program in memory.

**MID$** *(string, N, M)*

Returns M characters from *string* beginning at position N.

**MKD$** *(double prec.)*

Converts double precision value to a string.

**MKI$** *(integer)*

Converts integer value to string.

**MKS$** *(single prec.)*

Converts single precision value to a string.

**NAME** *filespec* **AS** *filename*

Used to rename a diskette file.

**NEW**

Erases current program and variables in RAM.

**OCT$** *(argument)*

Returns octal value of its *argument*.

**ON ERROR GOTO** *line*

Allows error trapping routine. When an error is encountered, the program will branch to the specified line number.

**ON** *expression* **GOSUB** *line...*

Transfers control to indicated subroutine.

**ON** *expression* **GOTO** *line...*

Transfers control to indicated line.

**OPEN** *mode* , [#] *filenumber, filespec,* [*rcd length*]

The OPEN command is used to open a disk file prior to any input or output operations. The OPEN statement the mode under which the file will be accessed. The OPEN statement also assigns an I/O buffer to the file.

The *mode* can be any one of the following:

| | |
|---|---|
| O | Sequential output mode |
| I | Sequential input mode |
| R | Random input/output mode |

*Filenumber* is a number that will be associated with the file as long as that file is open. *Filenumber* can range from 1 to 15.

*Filespec* identifies the name of the file being opened and optionally its drive identifier as well.

*Rcd length* is an optional parameter which can be used to set the record length for random access files. The default value for the record length of random access files is 128 bytes.

**OPTION BASE** *N*

Specifies a minimum value for array subscripts.

**OUT** *port, byte*

Sends specified *byte* to a machine output *port*.

**PEEK** (*N*)

Used to read a byte from the memory location specified by *N*.

**POKE** *address, byte*

Used to write a byte to a specified memory location.

**POS** *(argument)*

Returns the cursor column position. The argument has no effect on the value returned.

**PRINT** [*expressions*] $\begin{bmatrix} ; \\ , \end{bmatrix}$...

Used to display the data given in *expressions* on the screen. If no *expressions* are indicated, a blank line will be output.

One or several *expressions* can be included as PRINT statement parameters. If several *expressions* are included, each of the *expresions* must be delimited with either a comma, a semicolon, or a blank space. If a comma is used as a delimiter, the next *expression* will be output in the screen's next print zone (explained in the next paragraph). A semicolon causes the next *expression* to be output immediately after the preceding *expression*. The use of a blank space as a delimiter has the same effect as a semicolon.

In Microsoft BASIC, the output line is divided into print zones of 14 spaces each. As mentioned previously, if a comma is used as a delimiter, the *expression* following the comma will be output in the print zone following that used for the preceding *expression*.

If a PRINT statement is ended with a comma, the next PRINT statement will begin printing on the same output line at the next print zone. If a PRINT statement is ended with a semicolon, the next PRINT statement will begin printing on the same output line at the next available print position.

**PRINT USING** *"string"; expressions*

Used to display string or numeric data in a pre-defined format. This format is specified in the *string* parameter specified in the PRINT USING statement.

**PRINT#** *filenumber, expressions*

Writes data to the specified sequential disk file. The data to be written is indicated in *expressions*.

**PRINT#** *filenumber,* **USING** *"string"; expressions*

Writes data to file specified using the format specified in *string*. The data to be written is indicated in *expressions*.

**PUT** *filenumber* [*, recordnumber*]

Writes a specified record from a random buffer to a random file.

**RANDOMIZE** [*argument*]

Resets the random number generator. If no parameter is specified, RANDOMIZE will prompt the operator for a numeric entry which will be used as the seed for the random number generator.

**READ** variable [,...]

Reads values specified by the DATA statement and assigns these values to the *variables* specified.

**REM** *remark*

Used to include remarks in the program.

**RENUM** [[*argument1*][,[*argument2*], [*increment*]]

Used to renumber program lines. Renumbering begins at the line specified in *argument 2*. The numbers begin with the value specified in *argument 1* and increase by the *increment* value for each subsequent line.

**RESTORE** [*line*]

Used to reset the DATA statement pointer.

**RESUME** [*line*]

Used to continue program execution after execution of an error recovery routine.

**RETURN**

Returns program control from a subroutine.

**RIGHT$** *(string, N)*

Returns the N rightmost characters of *string*.

**RND** [*argument*]

Used to return a random number.

**RUN** [*"filespec"*]

Used to execute the program currently stored in memory.

**SAVE** *"filespec"* [,A][,P]

Used to save a BASIC program on diskette.

The A option is used to store the program in the ASCII format. This is necessary if programs are intended to be MERGE'd.

The P option prevents the program from being LIST'ed or EDIT'ed in the future.

**SGN** *(argument)*

Returns the sign of its *argument*.

**SIN** *(argument)*

Returns the sine of the angle given in *argument* which must be in *radians*.

**SPACE$** (*N*)

Returns a string consisting of the number of blank spaces specified.

**SPC** (*N*)

Prints the number of spaces specified. SPC can only be used with PRINT and LPRINT.

**SQR** *(argument)*

Returns the square root of the *argument*.

**STOP**

Used to stop program execution, print a break message, and return to command level.

**STR$** *(argument)*

Returns the string representation of the *argument*.

**STRING$** *(N, string)*

The first character of the specified *string* is returned the number of times specified in N.

**SWAP** *variable, variable*

Exchange values between 2 variables.

**TAB** (*N*)

Used to tab to position N in a PRINT or LPRINT statement.

**TAN** *(argument)*

Returns the tangent of the angle given in *argument,* which must be in radians.

**TROFF**

Used to turn off trace flag.

**TRON**

Used to set the trace flag which prints the line number of each statement in the program as it is executed.

**USR** *N (argument)*

Calls the machine language subroutine specified.

**VAL** *(string)*

Returns the numeric value of its string argument.

**VARPTR** *(variable)*

Returns the address of the *variable* in memory.

**WAIT** *port, mask*

Halts program execution until *port* specified develops specified bit pattern.

**WHILE** *expression...statements...***WEND**

Executes a series of statements as long as *expression* evaluates as true.

**WIDTH** *N*

Used to set output line width.

**WRITE** *expression...*

Used to display data on the screen.

**WRITE#** *filenumber, expression*

Used to output data to a file.

# CHAPTER 10. S-BASIC OVERVIEW

## INTRODUCTION

In this chapter, we will provide an overview of S-BASIC, a version of BASIC supplied with the Kaypro computer. This chapter is not meant to be a tutorial on BASIC programming. That subject in itself warrants a separate book.

S-BASIC programs are written as source programs or source code. Source code consists of the S-BASIC reserved words such as INPUT, PRINT, READ, and DATA, variable names, operators, and functions organized into meaningful program statements. The source code is the form of BASIC generally dealt with by programmers.

S-BASIC converts the source code into a set of instructions that can be executed directly by the computer. This conversion process is known as **compilation**. The series of symbols that can be executed by the computer is known as the **object code**. The object code is stored in a file with the same filename as that specified in the source code, but with a filename extension of .COM.

The advantage of a compiled version of BASIC lies in the fact that the object code contains instructions that can be readily understood by the computer. Interpretation is not necessary, and therefore, the program execution will be much faster. Fast execution can be a real advantage when a complex applications program is being run.

Unfortunately, the compiling of a S-BASIC program can be a time consuming procedure. As a result, debugging a compiled program is very inconvenient. Each time a program is edited, the compilation procedure must be repeated. This can become a time consuming and frustrating task.

**Creating and Editing Files**

Generally, S-BASIC programs are written with the Perfect Writer program. This allows the user to benefit from the editing features of the word processor.

Unfortunately, the S-BASIC compiler and other S-BASIC programs are on the CP/M diskette. These compiler programs must be present on one of the diskettes each time an S-BASIC program is compiled or executed.

As a result, program files should be stored on a diskette in drive B, and drive A should be available for the Perfect Writer or CP/M diskette. When a program is being edited, insert the Perfect Writer diskette in drive A. When programs are being compiled or executed, use the CP/M diskette in drive A.

For example, begin by using the word processor to create a program file on the diskette in drive B. Proceed by removing the Perfect Writer diskette and inserting the CP/M diskette in drive A. The program can now be compiled and executed. If the program needs to be edited, be sure to insert the Perfect Writer diskette in drive A once again.

If you do not wish to swap diskettes each time the program needs to be edited, you may copy the essential files from the CP/M diskette onto a blank diskette. This allows programs to be edited and executed without swapping diskettes.

To begin this procedure, insert the CP/M diskette in drive A, and a blank, formatted diskette in drive B. Press the Reset switch, and execute the PIP command in response to the system prompt (A>).

A><u>PIP</u> ↵

When the asterisk appears on the display, enter each of the following statements. After the Return key has been pressed, an asterisk will appear automatically at the next line.

```
* B:=A:SBASIC.COM
* B:=A:*.BAS
* B:=A:USERLIB.REL
* B:=A:BASICLIB.REL
* B:=A:OVERLAYB.COM
*
```

When the Return key is used in response to the prompt (*), a Warm Boot will be performed and the system prompt will be displayed.

When the PIP command is complete, the diskette in drive B will contain all the programs necessary to use S-BASIC. However, the diskette has nearly 100K of additional capacity to store S-BASIC programs.

If the Perfect Writer diskette remains in drive A, and the newly created S-BASIC diskette remains in drive B, the S-BASIC language can be used without swapping diskettes.

## The Compiler Filename Extension

A special filename extension must be used in S-BASIC during the compilation process. The three letters in the "compiler filename extension" are used to select the following three options.

- The drive where the source code is stored. (A or B)
- The drive where the object code is to be stored. (A or B)
- The drive or device where the print file is to be listed (A or B indicate a drive; X indicates the console; Y indicates the list device)

## Compiling S-BASIC Programs

The SBASIC command is used to compile an S-BASIC program. When the source code of a program is stored in a diskette file, the SBASIC command will be used to create an object code file. The object code is simply a compilation of the source code.

The SBASIC command can only be used when the system prompt (B>) appears on the display. The name of the source code file must be included in the SBASIC command. Even though all S-BASIC source code files must have the filename extension .BAS, the "compiler filename extension" must be used when the SBASIC command is executed.

For example, consider the S-BASIC program (source code) PROGRAM.BAS. The source code for this program should be created on the diskette in drive B with Perfect Writer. Be sure that the S-BASIC diskette is inserted in drive B.

Enter the following sample program in the file B: PROGRAM.BAS.

```
VAR A=INTEGER
WHILE A<100 DO
   BEGIN
       A=A+1
       PRINT A
   END
```

When Perfect Writer is exited and the system prompt (A>) appears on the display, execute the following command.

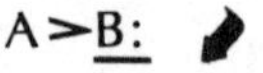


Since all of the S-BASIC programs are on the diskette in drive B, make drive B the default drive. The system prompt should now appear as B> rather than A>.

The following command begins the compilation.

```
B>SBASIC PROGRAM.BBX
```

Although the source code file has the filename extension .BAS, the "compiler filename extension" must be used with the SBASIC command. The three letters of this filename extension are used to specify the following three options.

- B The source file PROGRAM.BAS is located in the diskette in drive B.
- B The object file PROGRAM.COM will be stored on the diskette in drive B.
- X The results of the compilation will appear on the display.

When the SBASIC command is executed, the following information wil be displayed on the monitor.

```
         tm
S-BASIC Compiler Version 5.4b

0001:00  VAR A=INTEGER
0002:00  WHILE A<100 DO
0003:00    BEGIN
0004:01      A=A+1
0005:01      PRINT A
0006:01    END
0007:00          ****** End of program ******

Compilation complete
```

This information is the result of the compilation of the source code. If any of the statements in the source code do not have the correct format, the errors will be listed in the summary of the compilation results. If there are no problems in the format of the source code, the "compilation complete" message will be displayed.

When the compilation has been completed, a file that contains the object code will be stored on the diskette in drive B. The name of the object code file will be PROGRAM .COM.

The object code can be executed by specifying the filename (without the extension). The object code can only be executed when the system prompt (B>) is displayed. When the program is executed, the numbers from 1 to 100 will be displayed on the monitor.

To execute the sample program, execute the following command.

B>PROGRAM

If the program needs to be edited, the Perfect Writer program can be accessed by executing the following command.

B>A:PW PROGRAM.BAS

**S-BASIC Statement Structure**

The configurations of S-BASIC statements are described in this section with the following notation.

> Reserved words are in all capital letters.
> Optional items are enclosed in brackets. [ ]
> Parameters are presented in *italics*.
> Elipsis (...) represents repetition.
> Braces { } denote that a choice of items are available.

Unlike the other popular versions of BASIC, S-BASIC does not require a line number with each statement. Generally, line numbers are only used if a statement is referenced in a GOTO or GOSUB statement.

A valid S-BASIC line number can consist of a digit (0-9) followed by any number of characters. Generally, integers should be used as line numbers.

## SBASIC Variable Types

The six different variable types that are used in S-BASIC are listed in Table 10-1.

**Table 10-1. Variable Types and Abbreviations**

| Variable Type | Abbreviation |
|---|---|
| REAL | RS |
| REAL.DOUBLE | RD |
| FIXED | F |
| INTEGER | I |
| STRING | S |
| CHAR | C |

The REAL variable type allows the usage of numbers with 6 digits of accuracy and a floating decimal point. If the number is larger than 6 digits, scientific notation is used. The following are examples of numbers that could be associated with REAL variables:

7.123     −3.98521     6.7534E+10

The REAL.DOUBLE variable type is similar to the REAL variable type. However, REAL.DOUBLE variables have 14 digits of accuracy rather than 6. The following are examples of numbers that can be associated with REAL.DOUBLE variables.

1.79354832124     7.932159347E4

Although REAL.DOUBLE variables allow more accuracy, they also require additional memory storage area.

The FIXED variable type is associated with values that have 8 digits to the left, and 3 digits to the right of the decimal point. However, only 2 of the 3 digits to the right of the decimal point are actually displayed. The following are examples of numbers that can be associated with FIXED variables:

8.73    99.42    11117.01

If a FIXED variable is assigned a value that either too large or too small, an error message will be generated. When FIXED variable type numbers are printed, they are automatically aligned around the decimal point. The FIXED variable type is especially useful for working with numbers in a dollar and cents format.

The INTEGER variable type allows the usage of values between +32767 and -32767. No decimal portion is allowed. Integer values require less memory storage area than any other type of number value.

The STRING variable type can include any of the ASCII characters. Up to 255 characters including numbers, letters, spaces, and special characters can be assigned to a string variable.

A CHAR variable can be assigned a single ASCII character. Any letter, number or special character can be assigned to a CHAR variable.

**Variable Declaration Statements**

Before a variable can be used in an S-BASIC program it must first be declared. A variable declaration statement is used to indicate the variable's name, type and location within the computer's memory.

Generally, variables may be stored in either of two different areas in memory. They may be stored in the data storage area (an area reserved by the SBASIC compiler) or the common storage area (an area where variables will not be changed during the chaining of various S-BASIC programs).

**VAR or VARIABLE**

The VAR statement is used to declare variables which are to be stored in the data storage area. VAR uses the following format:

*VAR *variable name, ...= type* [:*size*]

The six variable *types* were discussed in the preceding section and are listed in Table 10-1.

*Size* is an optional parameter which indicates the size of a STRING variable. *Size* may range from 1 to 255 characters with a default value of 80.

Examples of S-BASIC VAR statements are given below:

```
VAR A = REAL
VAR PAY = INTEGER
VAR EMPL.NAME = STRING:30
```

In the first example, A is declaraed as a REAL variable. In the second example, PAY is declared as an INTEGER variable. In the the third example, EMPL.NAME is declared a STRING variable with a maximum length of 30 characters. All of the VAR statements allocate storage space in the data storage area.

---

* VAR and VARIABLE may be used interchangeably.

## COM or COMMON

The COM or COMMON statement is used to declare variables which are to be stored in the common storage area of memory. The following configuration is used for the COM statement:

*COM *variable name,...=type* [:*size*]

## DIM or DIMENSION

The DIM statement is used to allocate memory space for an array. DIM is used with the following configuration:

*DIM [ COM ] *type* [:*length*] *array name* (*size*)...

If COM is specified, the array is stored in the common storage area. If COM is not specified, then the array is stored in the data storage area.

*Type* denotes the type of variable being dimensioned. If an array contains string values, the *length* parameter can be used to determine the maximum number of characters in each string. The *array name* parameter is used to specify the variable name of the array. The number of elements in the array are specified by *size*.

The following are examples of the use of the DIM statement:

```
DIM INTEGER X(5,5)
DIM COM REAL Y(3,4)
```

In the first example, array X is dimensioned in the data storage area. Array X can be assigned 36 INTEGER elements.

---

* COM and COMMON may be used interchangeably. Either DIM or DIMENSION can be used.

In the second example, array Y is declared a COMMON variable. Array Y can be assigned 20 REAL values. The values designated by the variable names Y(0,0) through Y(3,4).

## LOCATION

The LOCATION statement can be used to determine the location of a data item. LOCATION uses the following configuration:

$$\text{LOCATION} \left\{ \begin{matrix} \text{VAR} \\ \text{ARRAY} \\ \text{FILE} \end{matrix} \right\} \textit{variable 1= variable 2}$$

LOCATION can be used to determine the address of a variable (VARIABLE), array (ARRAY), or disk input/output buffer (FILE). *Variable* will be set to the memory address of *variable.*

## Block Structures

A **block structure** is a group of statements which is treated as a single logical statement. The BEGIN and END statements can be used to denote the beginning and end of a block structure. The following group of statements is considered a single logical statement.

```
BEGIN
  VAR A=REAL
  A=B*C
  PRINT SQR(A)
END
```

Variables may be declared within a block structure with a VAR statement. However, those variables are only declared within the block structure. Outside the block structure, they are considered undeclared.

### Assignment Statements

An assignment statement is one that determines the value of an expression and then assigns that result to the variable named in the assignment statement. The LET statement is an optional keyword that can be used in an assignment statement.

The configuration of an assignment statement is given below:

[LET]*variable=expression*

The variable must be of the same data type as the expression. For example, if the variable is a string, the expression must also be a string.

## ARITHMETIC OPERATIONS

The following arithmetic operations are used in S-BASIC: addition, subtraction, multiplication, division, and exponentation. Symbols are used in S-BASIC to represent these arithmetic operations.

The symbols + and - represent addition and subtraction respectively. The slash (/) represents division and the asterisk (*) represents multiplication.

An arithmetic operation or a series of operations which are grouped together are known as an **expression.** The following are examples of arithmetic expressions.

```
1 + 2
X + Y - Z
(A*B) + C
A * B - 7
```

As you can see from the preceding examples, arithmetic expressions may include constants, variables, or both.

### Unary Operator

The minus sign (-) is used to indicate subtraction, but it can also be used to change the sign of a value. When the minus sign is used in this manner, it is called a unary operator because it operates on only one value.

A unary minus can be used to change the sign of an integer or real variable, as shown in the example below.

AMOUNT.PAID=-AMOUNT.PAID

### Exponentiation

The raising of a number to a power is known as exponentiation. For example, 2 raised to the power of 4 is equal to 16. In algebra, this is represented as:

$$2^4=16$$

In S-BASIC, a carat (^) or double asterisk (**) can be used to represent exponentiation.

## RELATIONAL OPERATIONS

S-BASIC uses the following six relational operators.

1. Less than (<)
2. Greater than (>)
3. Equal to (=)
4. Less than, or equal to (<=)
5. Greater than, or equal to (>=)
6. Not equal (< >)

A relational comparison results in either a condition of true or false. For example, the following relational comparison would be considered true.

7 > 5

The relational comparison below would be considered false.

5 > 7

When S-BASIC evaluates a relational comparison, it returns a value of -1 if the comparison is true, and a value of 0 is the comparison is false.

These results of a relational comparison (0 and -1) are known as **logical** values. S-BASIC logical values are handled as integer data items. This means that when a relational comparison is set up, the result will be an integer.

The following examples illustrate the values returned by S-BASIC for relational comparisons.

7 < 3 = 0 (false)
5 > 2 = -1 (true)
100>99 = -1 (true)
100 = 100 = -1 (true)

## LOGICAL OPERATORS

A logical or Boolean operator evaluates an input of one or more operands with true or false values. The logical operator evaluates these true or false values and returns a value of true or false. The result of a logical operation is considered true if it has a non-zero value. (Remember, relational operators return a value of –1 for a true value.) The result of a logical operation is considered false if it is equal to zero.

The result of a logical operation is a number. Non-zero values are considered true, and zero values are considered false. Logical or Boolean operations are generally used in S-BASIC to compare the results of two relational operations. Logical operations return a true or false value which can be used to determine program flow. The following example demonstrates this concept.

If X > 10 or Y < 0 THEN GOTO 900

There are six logical operators that can be used in S-BASIC. Five of these operators are binary (require two arguments), and one is unary (only one argument). The results of the logical operators are summarized in Tables 10-2 and 10-3.

**Table 10-2. The Binary Logical Operators**

| X | Y | X AND Y | X OR Y | X XOR Y | X IMP Y | X EQV Y |
|---|---|---|---|---|---|---|
| T | T | T | T | F | T | T |
| F | T | F | T | T | T | F |
| T | F | F | T | T | F | F |
| F | F | F | F | F | T | T |

**Table 10-3. The NOT Operator**

| X | NOT X |
|---|---|
| T | F |
| F | T |

## Order of Evaluation of Expressions

When several operators are used in an expression, the order of evaluation of the operators is important. For example, the expression 2 + 3 * 4 can be equal to 20 or 14, depending upon the order in which the operations are performed.

Table 10-4 contains a summary of the "priority levels" among operators. The operations in an expression are performed from the highest priority to the lowest. Operators that have the same priority level are performed from right to left in the expression.

**Table 10-4. Operator Priority Levels**

| | |
|---|---|
| Highest priority | Expressions enclosed in parenthesis |
| | Exponentiation |
| | Unary minus |
| | Multiplication and Division |
| | Addition and Subtraction |
| | Relational operators |
| Lowest priority | Boolean operators |

## PROGRAM CONTROL STATEMENTS

In S-BASIC, program execution generally flows from one statement to the next. However, a number of program control statements are available in S-BASIC for diverting this normal execution pattern. These will be discussed in the following sections.

### GOTO

This statement transfers control to the indicated line number (ex. GOTO 200).

### GOSUB

The GOSUB statement transfers program control to the statement with the specified line number. After the subroutine has been executed and a RETURN statement is encountered, control will return to the statement following the GOSUB statement.

### ON...GOTO

The ON...GOTO statement can be used to branch program control to any of several statements. The following configuration is used for ON...GOTO:

ON *integer expression* GOTO *statement number* [,...]

The value of the *integer expression* determines the statement to which program control branches.

ON X GOTO 1000, 2000, 3000

In the preceding example, program control will branch to 1000, 2000, or 3000 if X is equal to 1, 2, or 3 respectively.

**ON...GOSUB**

An ON...GOSUB statement is very similar to an ON...GOTO statement. However, the ON...GOSUB statement branches the program control to a subroutine rather than to a line number.

When the subroutine is complete, a RETURN statement will cause the program control to return to the statement immediately following the ON...GOSUB statement.

**ON ERROR**

S-BASIC errors can either be fatal (program execution is stopped) or non-fatal (execution is not stopped). Fatal errors cause program control to be transferred to the operating system. Non-fatal errors cause an error message to be printed, but execution is not stopped.

The ON ERROR statement is generally used to transfer program control to a specified line number when a fatal error is encountered. ON ERROR is generally used with the following configuration:

ON ERROR GOTO *line number*

An ON ERROR statement is active throughout an S-BASIC program until another ON ERROR statement is encountered.

**REPEAT...UNTIL**

A REPEAT...UNTIL loop uses the following configuration:

REPEAT *program statement* UNTIL *expression*

The specified *statements* will be repeated until the given *expression* becomes true. Remember, a block structure is evaluated as a simple program statement. An example of a REPEAT...UNTIL loop is given below.

```
VAR X=INTEGER
REPEAT
  BEGIN
    X=X + 1
    PRINT X
  END
UNTIL X > 10
```

**WHILE...DO**

The WHILE...DO statement is also used to transfer program control. WHILE...DO loops use the following configuration:

WHILE *expression* DO *program statement*

As long as the *expression* is true (non-zero) the specified *program statement* will be performed.

**CASE...END**

The CASE...END statement allows program control to be transferred to one program statement from a choice of several statements. CASE...END statements use the following configuration:

CASE *expression* OF
*expression 1*: *program statement 1*
*expression 2*: *program statement 2*
⋮
*expression x*: *program statement x*
END

If the *expression* equals *expression 1,* then *program statement 1* is executed. If the *expression* equals *expression 2, program statement 2* is executed.

**IF...THEN**

The configuration for IF THEN ELSE is shown below.

If *expression* THEN *statement* [ELSE *statement*]

If the expression following IF is true, the statement following THEN will be executed. If the expression is not true, the statements following ELSE will be executed.

**FOR...NEXT**

The FOR NEXT statement is used to re-execute a set of statements a specified number of times.

The FOR statement is used to begin the FOR/NEXT loop. The FOR statement sets an index value which keeps track of how many times the loop is performed. The FOR statement also sets a limit as to the number of times the loop is to be performed. The configuration for NEXT is given below.

FOR *variable* = *expression 1* TO *expression 2* [STEP *expression 3*]
:
NEXT

The variable following the FOR statement is known as the index. The index must be a variable, but it cannot be an element of an array. The numeric expression following the equal sign is evaluated and initially assigned to the index variable. The numeric expression after TO is the maximum index value.

The expression after STEP is the value by which the index variable's value is to be increased or decreased following each run through the FOR...NEXT loop (iteration). This expression is known as the increment. After each iteration, the increment is calculated and then added to the present index variable value. The index variable value is then compared to the final index variable value (after the TO).

The looping will continue until the index variable value exceeds the final index value. If no value is specified for the increment, the value of the index variable increases by 1 each time the loop is iterated.

## S-BASIC INPUT/OUTPUT STATEMENTS

Input/Output (I/O) statements are designed to retrieve data from the keyboard, disk drive, or some other input device or to output data to the display, printer or some other output device. The principle S-BASIC I/O statements are INPUT, PRINT and TEXT. Each of these will be discussed in the following sections.

### I/O Devices

The various physical devices have pre-assigned channel numbers in S-BASIC. These assignments are listed in Table 10-5.

**Table 10-5. I/O Device Channel Assignments**

| Channel # | Input Device | Output Device |
|---|---|---|
| 0 | Console | Console |
| 1 | Dummy* | List |
| 2 | Dummy* | Punch |
| 3 | Reader | Dummy* |
| 4 | Console Status | Dummy* |
| 5 | Keyin | Keyout (Dummy)* |

*Dummy refers to a nonexistent device.

## INPUT

The INPUT statement is used to retrieve data from the console or another input device and to assign that data to a specified variable. INPUT uses the following configuration:

INPUT[#*channel*;][“*prompt*” {; ,} ]*variable*[,...]

#*channel* specifies the input channel number. If #*channel* is not specified, the console (device 0) will be used.

The *prompt* message is a string which is to be displayed on the console before data is accepted. The *prompt* message is optional.

If a *prompt* message is used, either a comma (,) or a semicolon (;) must follow *prompt* in the INPUT statement. If the semicolon is used, INPUT will request data entry immediately after the prompt message. If the comma is used, INPUT will request data entry at the next tab position. Tab positions occur after every 14 columns in the display.

At least one *variable* must be specified with the INPUT statement. The data entered in response to the INPUT prompt will be assigned to the specified *variable*(*s*). The variable names in an INPUT statement must be separated by commas.

Note that more than one *variable* can be specified within a single INPUT statement. If this is the case, more than one data item must be entered since each *variable* requires a data item entry.

When a single INPUT statement is used to assign values to several variables, the values that are input must be separated by commas.

If an INPUT statement is used to assign a string value to a single string variable, commas can be included in the string data. However, if an INPUT statement is used to assign values to two or more string variables, commas must be used to separate the values. In this situation, if it is necessary to include a comma in a string, the value must be enclosed in quotation marks. This principle is demonstrated in Illustration 10-1.

**Illustration 10-1. Assigning String Values with INPUT Statements**

| INPUT Statement | Response | Values |
|---|---|---|
| INPUT A | JONES, BILL | A=JONES, BILL |
| INPUT A, B | JONES, BILL | A=JONES<br>B=BILL |
| INPUT A,B | "JONES, BILL","SMITH, JIM" | A=JONES, BILL<br>B=SMITH, JIM |

### PRINT

The PRINT statement is used to send OUTPUT to a device. PRINT utilizes the following configuration:

PRINT [#*channel*;][*data* {, ;} *data*...]

*Channel* refers to the I/O channel to which the PRINT statement output is to be directed. If no channel is specified, the output is sent to the monitor (channel 0).

A PRINT statement can include string and numeric variables, as well as string and numeric constants. Each variable name or constant must be separated by either a comma or a semicolon. When a comma separates the items in a PRINT statement, the values are displayed in columns. When a semicolon is used between items in a PRINT statement, the values are displayed adjacent to each other, with one space preceding numeric values.

A PRINT statement can end with a comma, semicolon, or no punctuation at all. A PRINT statement that ends with a semicolon causes the cursor to wait at the next position until another PRINT statement is executed. The cursor waits at the next available column when a PRINT statement ends with a comma. When a PRINT statement has no punctuation at the end, the next item occurs on the next line.

## CONSOLE and LPRINTER

As mentioned in the preceding section, the default device for the PRINT statement's output is the console (channel 0). The LPRINTER statement can be used to change the default device to the printer (channel 1). The CONSOLE statement can be executed to change the default output device back to the console (device 0).

## TEXT

The TEXT statement is used to send large blocks of text to a specified device. Generally, TEXT is more convenient for this purpose than is the PRINT statement. TEXT uses the following configuration:

TEXT *channel, delimiter 1 text delimiter 2;*[ ; ]
                                                          [ , ]

*channel* indicates the I/O channel where the data is to be output. The *text* to be output is set off by 2 *delimiters.* These *delimiters* can be any character. However, the character used for the *delimiters* must not be used in the *text. Delimiter 1* and *delimiter 2* must be identical. The use of the comma and semicolon to end the statement follow the same conventions described in PRINT.

The following is an example of the use of a TEXT statement.

```
TEXT 1, %
     Weber Systems Inc.
     8437 Mayfield Rd.
     Chesterland, Ohio %
```

Notice in the preceding example that the data is output to the printer (device #1), and that the percent sign (%) is used as the delimiter.

**PRINT USING**

The PRINT USING statement is used to output data in a predetermined format to the indicated device. PRINT USING statements have the following configuration.

PRINT USING *"string expression"* [#*channel*;] *data,...*

The string expression following the PRINT USING statement is the format string. This consists of literal characters and data templates. Literal characters are to be printed exactly as they appear in the string expression. Data templates describe the format that will be used to output the data in the PRINT USING statement.

An example of literal characters would be the expression, "The total cost is". An example of data template characters would be "$$#,###.##".

The following characters are used as data templates:

- . Decimal point.
- , Comma—requires comma insertion every three digits before the decimal point.
- # Indicates position of one digit in the numeric output.
- ^\ Indicates a number in exponential format.
- ** Fills field with leading asterisks.
- $$ Places floating dollar sign at the beginning of numeric data.
- ! Outputs first character of a string value.

& Outputs the entire string value.

/ Indicates the beginning and end of string field.

\ Indicates that the next character in the format expression is to be treated as a literal character.

\+ Indicates the sign of the number being output. This character may be indicated either at the beginning or the end of the format string. A + will be printed if the number is positive; a - if negative.

\- Functions just like the + character except that if the number is positive a blank space is printed rather than a +.

The #*channel* indicates the device to which the data is to be output. *Data* specifies the information to be output. *Data* can consist of numeric or string constants and/or variables.

Table 10-6 includes several example PRINT USING statements as well as the corresponding output.

**Table 10-6. Example PRINT USING Statements**

| Statement | Result |
|---|---|
| PRINT USING "$$#,###.##";5381.685 | $5,381.69 |
| PRINT USING "##.##—";—6.19 | 6.19— |
| PRINT USING "#.## ∧ ∧ ∧ ∧";489.1 | 489E+2 |
| PRINT USING "/../";"JOHNSON" | JOHN |
| PRINT USING "Cost $$##.##";24.95 | Cost   $24.95 |

## S-BASIC DISK FILE ACCESS

**File Access** refers to the means by which information can be placed in or retrieved from a data storage medium such as a floppy diskette. The following sections contain an explanation of the file access procedures used in S-BASIC.

The diskette surface can be visualized as being divided into the following three areas:

System Area
Directory Area
Data Storage Area

The System area is that portion of the diskette where the operating system (CP/M) is stored. The directory area is used to store disk directory information.

The disk directory is a file which contains a catalog of the files stored on the diskette. When a file is created, deleted, or renamed, the disk directory will be altered to reflect these changes.

The data storage area is the portion of the diskette where data and program files are written.

Different S-BASIC statements affect these different areas of the diskette. For instance, certain S-BASIC statements are used to initialize memory I/O buffers for the operating system. These buffers are used for transferring data during disk read and write operations. Other S-BASIC statements are available to create or delete directory entries. Finally, S-BASIC also includes statements which are used to transfer data to and from the diskette.

## Random and Sequential File Access

Two different types of disk files can be used with S-BASIC. These two types are called random and sequential files.

The important difference between random and sequential files is the way in which each file is accessed. **Direct Access** of any record in a random file is possible regardless of that record's location within the file.

By direct access, we mean that any record in the file may be retrieved regardless of its position, without having to search through the entire file to find it.

Records in a sequential file can only be retrieved by **sequential access.** In sequential access, the record search begins with the first record in the file and must continue until the desired record is found.

In other words, in a sequential file, to find record 17, S-BASIC would first have to read the first 16 records, one by one. Since S-BASIC does not know the record length of sequential files, it has no way of determining the location of record 17, other than by reading the first 16 records.

With random files, S-BASIC knows the length of each record and easily can calculate the location of any record on the file.

Both random and sequential files have advantages and disadvantages other than file access. Sequential files use less disk space than random files. Since each record in a sequential file is assigned only the disk space it needs, no diskette space is wasted by sequential files. Random files require every record to be assigned the same amount of disk space required by the longest record in that file. This generally results in wasted space in random files.

Random files have an advantage over sequential files in that a record from a random file may be read into memory, changed, and then written back to the disk. A record from a sequential file cannot be read, modified, and then rewritten, because any change that might affect a single record's length would affect the entire file.

## CREATE, DELETE, RENAME

CREATE, DELETE and RENAME are used to change entries in the disk directory. CREATE is used to create an entry in the directory. CREATE uses the following configuration:

CREATE"*filename*"

The *filename* specified will be entered in the directory. CREATE does not affect the data storage area of the diskette.

DELETE causes the specified file to be deleted from the directory. Any data stored in association with this filename will be erased. DELETE uses the following configuration:

DELETE"*filename*"

RENAME is used to change a file's name. The data in the file is not affected by RENAME. RENAME is used with the following configuration:

RENAME"*filename 1*" TO "*filename 2*"

The file specified in *filename 1* will be renamed to the name indicated by *filename 2*.

**INITIALIZE**

Whenever diskettes are changed under S-BASIC, the INITIALIZE statement must be executed. INITIALIZE is used to reset the disk directory maps for the operating system. This allows diskettes to be swapped during program execution without having to restart the operating system.

**FILES Statement**

All disk input and output is accomplished through file channels. These channels are defined with the FILES statement. The FILES statement uses the following configuration:

$$\text{FILES}\begin{Bmatrix}\text{S}\\\text{R}\end{Bmatrix}(\textit{size}),\ldots$$

If S is indicated, the channel is initialized for sequential file access. *Size* will specify the size of the I/O buffer for this channel in sectors.

If R is indicated, the channel is initialized for random file access. *Size* indicates the number of bytes per record. It is recommended that *size* be a multiple of 128, as records of this size are accessed more quickly.

Only one FILES statement is allowed per program. As many as 32 channels may be opened with a single FILES statement. An example of a FILES statement is given below:

```
FILES R(256), S(2), S(3)
```

In the preceding example, channel 0 is opened for random access with a record size of 2 sectors or 256 bytes. Channel 1 is opened for sequential access with a buffer length of 2 sectors. Channel 2 is also opened for serial access with a buffer length of 3 sectors.

**OPEN**

The OPEN statement assigns a file channel (initialized with the FILES statement) to a diskette file. OPEN is used with the following configuration:

OPEN #*channel*; "*filename*"

*Channel* specifies a file channel initialized with the FILES statement. *Filename* specifies the file which is to be associated with the indicated channel number.

In the following example, TEXT.DAT is opened for access via channel 3.

```
OPEN #3;"TEXT.DAT"
```

**CLOSE**

When access to a file has been completed, that file should be closed with the CLOSE statement. CLOSE causes the disk buffer to be cleared and the directory to be updated to reflect any changes made to the file.

CLOSE uses the following configuration:

CLOSE #*channel*

The file associated with the specified *channel* in the OPEN statement will be closed. The indicated channel can than be used for a different file.

The following example statement could be used to close a file that was previously opened for channel 3.

CLOSE #3

**WRITE**

The WRITE statement is used to send output to a file. The configuration for WRITE is as follows:

WRITE #*channel; expression,...* ← Sequential Access

WRITE #*channel,rcd*;[*expressive*],... ← Random Access

In the sequential access configuration, *channel* specifies the file to which data is to be written. The file associated with that channel number in the OPEN statement will be the file to which data will be written.

Data will be written to a sequential file, one item at a time from the beginning of the file to its end. *Expression* specifies the data to be entered. *Expression* can either be a constant or a variable.

In the random access configuration, *channel* indicates the file to which data is to be written. *rcd* specifies the record number within the file where the data is to be written. The data indicated by *expression* will be written to the random access file record.

The following two examples demonstrate the correct format of WRITE statements.

WRITE #3;A ← Sequential Access

WRITE #1,2;A ← Random Access

## READ

Two different versions of the READ statement are available—one for sequential access and the other for random access.

READ #*channel*; *variable*,... ← Sequential Access

READ #*channel*, *rcd*; *variable*,... ← Random Access

In the sequential access configuration, data is read from the indicated *channel* into the specified *variables*. Before READ can be executed, an OPEN statement must first have been executed to associate a file with the indicated channel number.

In the random access configuration, the record number specified by *rcd* will be read from the file into a buffer. Data from this record can then be read into the indicated *variables*.

A random file can be read from and written to via the same channel. However, when a sequential file is written, the information cannot be recovered until the I/O channel is closed and another channel is opened for the same file.

## S-BASIC FUNCTIONS

S-BASIC allows for two different types of functions—built-in functions (i.e. LOC, TAN, SIN etc.) and user-defined functions. S-BASIC's built-in functions are summarized in Table 10-7. User-defined functions are discussed in the following sections.

## FUNCTION...END

User-defined functions are defined with the FUNCTION, END statement. This statement uses the following format:

FUNCTION *name* [(*argument*;...]=*type*
*body*
END=*expression*

*Name* specifies the function name.

*Argument* is an optional parameter. When a user-defined function is called from within an expression, the function may require that one or more arguments be passed to it. If this is the case, these arguments must be defined in the *argument* parameter portion of the FUNCTION statement. Notice that the *argument* parameter is enclosed in parentheses.

Generally, *argument* uses the same format as a VAR statement except that VAR need not be specified. The following are examples of valid *argument* parameters:

(X=REAL)
(A=INTEGER;B=REAL)

*Type* determines the data type of the result of the function. Any of the data types listed in Table 10-1 can be used as the *type* parameter.

*Body* consists of S-BASIC statements which are used to perform calculations within the function.

The END statement indicates the end of the S-BASIC user-defined function. The *expression* determines the value returned by the function. The type of value returned by the function is determined by the *type* parameter.

The following program demonstrates the use of a FUNCTION statement.

```
              VAR A=REAL
Function  {   FUNCTION COT (B=REAL)=REAL
              END=COS(B)/SIN(B)
              INPUT A
              PRINT COT (A)
```

This program is used to calculate the cotangent of an angle. The argument of the funciton must be a real number (because of the variable declaration B=REAL). The function returns a real number (because of the =REAL statement).

The value returned is calculated by the expression that follows the END statement. If more calculations are required in the function, S-BASIC statements can be included in the body of the function.

When the function is called in the last line of the program, the argument of the COT statement is used in place of the variable B in the function calculations. The function returns the value that is calculated in the last statement of the function.

**PROCEDURE...END**

A **procedure** can be defined as a subroutine to which variables can be passed when that procedure is called.

The configuration for a procedure is as follows:

PROCEDURE *name* [*argument*;...]
*body*
END

Note that the configuration for PROCEDURE is similar to that for FUNCTION, except that a *type* is not specified for a PROCEDURE, and that an *expression* is not included in the END statement.

The following example demonstrates the use of a procedure.

```
VAR A,B=REAL
PROCEDURE PERCENT (C,D=REAL)
    VAR X=REAL
    X=(C/D)*100
    PRINT C;"IS";X;"PERCENT OF ";D
END
INPUT A,B
PERCENT A,B
```

The example program uses the variables A and B throughout the program. However, the variable X is used only within the procedure. The variables C and D are dummy variables that are used to represent the values that are passed to the procedure.

When the procedure is called, the values that follow the procedure name are used in the calculations. The procedure calculates the ratio of the two values that are input, and returns the results in terms of a percentage.

**Table 10-7. S-BASIC Built-In Functions**

| Function Name | Function Description |
|---|---|
| ABS(*argument*) | This function returns the absolute value of its argument. |
| ASCII(*string*) | This function returns the ASCII code for the first character of its argument. |
| CHR$(*argument*) | Converts an ASCII code into its equivalent ASCII character. |
| COS(*argument*) | Returns the cosine of its *argument* (specified in radians). |
| EXP(*argument*) | Raise e (2.71828) to the power given in *argument*. |
| FCB$(*argument*) | Returns a string with a valid file control block format. |

**Table 10-7. S-BASIC Built-In Functions**

| Function Name | Function Description |
|---|---|
| FFIX(*argument*) | Returns the integer portion of a fixed type value. |
| FINT(*argument*) | Returns the next lowest integer which is less than or equal to its *argument*. |
| FIX(*argument*) | Truncates the *argument* and returns the integer portion. |
| FRE(*argument*) | If *argument* is false (0), the amount of free memory will be returned.<br><br>If *argument* is true, the number of blocks used on the current drive will be returned |
| HEX$(*argument*) | Converts its argument to an equivalent hexadecimal string. |
| INP(*argument*) | Returns the byte read from the port specified by *argument*. |
| INSTR(*n, string 1 string 2*) | INSTR searches for the initial appearance of one string (*string 1*) within another string (*string 2*). This search begins at the *n*th character within *string 2*. The position where the match occurs is returned by the function. If no match occurs, INSTR returns a value of 0. |
| INT(*argument*) | Returns the largest integer which is less than or equal to the *argument*. |
| LEFT$(*string,x*) | Returns the leftmost characters in the *string*. The number of characters returned is specified by *x*. |
| LEN(*string*) | Returns the length of the *string*. |

**Table 10-7. S-BASIC Built-In Functions**

| Function Name | Function Description |
|---|---|
| LOG(*argument*) | Returns the natural logarithm of the *argument.* |
| MID$(*string,c,* [*d*]) | Returns a portion of *string* beginning at the character position given in *c*. The number of characters to be returned is specified by *d.* |
| NUM$ (*argument*) | Returns a string equivalent of the *argument.* |
| PEEK*(address)* | Returns the contents of the memory location specified by *address.* |
| POS(*argument*) | This argument returns the current print position on the output channel if *argument* is positive. If *argument* is negative the current line count for the output channel is returned. |
| RIGHT$(*string,x*) | Returns the rightmost characters of *string* The number of characters to be returned is indicated by *x*. |
| RND(*argument*) | Returns a random number between 0 and 1 if *argument* is true. If *argument* is false, the last number generated will be returned. |
| SGN(*argument*) | Returns 1 if *argument* is greater than 0; 0 if *argument* is equal to 0; -1 if *argument* is less than 0. |
| SIN(*argument*) | Returns the sine of *argument* (given in radians). |
| SIZE(*argument*) | Returns the size of a disk file in blocks. |

**Table 10-7. S-BASIC Built-In Functions**

| Function Name | Function Description |
|---|---|
| SPACE$ (*argument*) | Returns a string consisting of the number of blank spaces indicated by *argument*. |
| SQR(*argument*) | Returns the square root of its *argument*. |
| STR$(*argument*) | Returns the string representation of the specified *argument*. |
| STRING$ (*b,c*) | Returns a string of length *b* which is composed of characters with an ASCII code equal to *c*. |
| TAN(*argument*) | Returns the tangent of *argument* (given in radians). |
| VAL(*argument*) | Returns the numeric value of its string *argument*. |
| XLATE(*string 1, string 2*) | Replaces the characters in *string 1* with the characters in *string 2*, based on ASCII values. For example, each dollar sign (ASCII 36) in *string 1* is converted to the 36th character of *string 2*. |

## Compiler Commands

Compiler commands are specific S-BASIC statements which instruct the compiler to undertake a special activity. Compiler commands do not actually affect program execution itself. They instead control the format of the listing produced by the compiler or control the compilation process itself.

Compiler commands can be easily identified. They begin with a dollar sign follwed by the name of the command. The various S-BASIC compiler commands will be discussed in the following sections.

**$LINES**

The LINES command can be used to suppress generation of line number references during compilation. If LINES is not executed, the compiler will print a line number along with an error message if a run-time error is encountered.

The production of line number references is suppressed by the inclusion of a $LINES statement. Once this compiler command has been executed, a run-time error will cause an error message to be output, but no line number reference will be specified.

**$PAGE**

The PAGE compiler command sends the ASCII form feed character to the list device (generally the printer). This causes the printer to proceed to a new page before the output continues.

**$TRACE**

The TRACE command causes line number references to be printed on the console during program execution. A separate line number reference is output for each S-BASIC statement. The following example includes a program as well as output that occurs as a result of the TRACE command.

```
$TRACE
VAR A,B,C=INTEGER
A=5
B=6
C=A*B
IF C>A+B THEN PRINT C,
END
```

```
[0002][0003][0004][0005][0006][0006]  30
[0007]
```

The TRACE command can be turned on or off during run time by entering Control-T at the console.

## $CONSTANT

The CONSTANT command is used to define an integer constant during compilation. This constant cannot be altered during the execution of the program.

The CONSTANT command uses the following configuration:

$CONSTANT *variable=value*

*Variable* indicates the variable being created. *Value* is the integer assigned to that variable.

The variable created by CONSTANT can be used in an expression like any other integer-type variable would be. The use of the CONSTANT command is demonstrated in the following example.

```
$CONSTANT MAX=100
```

## $LIST

The LIST command can be used to turn the listing of the source program from the compiler on or off. Initially, LIST is on. If $LIST is encountered in the source program, the listing feature will be turned off. If $LIST is encountered a second time, the listing will be turned back on.

## CHAIN

The CHAIN statement is used to transfer program control from the program currently being executed to the S-BASIC program specified. CHAIN uses the following configuration:

CHAIN "*filename*"

Where *filename* is the program to be chained. When the CHAIN statement is executed, the specified file will be loaded and that program will be executed. Only compiled versions of S-BASIC programs can be specified with the CHAIN statement (i.e. files with the extension .COM).

If variables are passed from the current program to the program being called with a CHAIN command, the variables must be declared with COMMON statements rather than VARIABLE statements.

Each program that is "chained" must have identical COMMON variable declarations. Also, the COMMON statements must be the first statements within each program.

The following example includes two programs that are "chained together."

```
COM X,Y=INTEGER          )
FOR X=1 TO 100           |
PRINT X                  |
NEXT X                   > PROGRAMA.BAS
CHAIN "B.COM"            |
END                      )

COM X,Y=INTEGER          )
FOR Y = X TO X + 100     |
PRINT Y                  > PROGRAMB.BAS
NEXT Y                   |
END                      )
```

Notice that the COM statements at the beginning of the programs are identical.

The CHAIN statement near the end of the first program is used to call the second program.

The output of the first program is the set of numbers from 1 to 100. The second program outputs the values from 100 to 200. The execution of the program pauses momentarily while the second program is accessed.

# INDEX



---

**Note to Reader:** Please note that for selected topics with several page references, one reference may be in bold type. The page noted in bold denotes the primary reference or definition of that topic.

# ABOUT THE WEBER SYSTEMS, INC. STAFF

In 1982, Weber Systems, Inc. began a start-up publishing division specializing in books related to the personal computer field. They initially published three books, and within a year, expanded their list to eighteen machine-specific titles, with fourteen more scheduled for early 1984.

All Weber Systems USER'S HANDBOOKS are created by an in-house editorial staff with extensive backgrounds in computer science and technical writing. The three basic tenets of their publishing philosophy are: quality, timeliness and maintenance (frequent updating).

Weber Systems is located in Cleveland, Ohio.

Other Books in This Series
Published by Ballantine Books

**IBM BASIC® USER'S HANDBOOK**
**IBM PC® & XT® USER'S HANDBOOK**
**VIC-20® USER'S HANDBOOK**